Praise for *Follo*[illegible]

"*Followed* is so much more than a guidebook for c[illegible] media. Sharing her own personal journey, Amanda Buc[illegible] offers a compassionate and trauma-informed perspective for anyone navigating our changing virtual landscape or looking to rediscover their authentic voice."

—Dr. Nicole LePera, #1 *New York Times* bestselling author of *How to Do the Work*

"This is the book I wish I had when I started making content! Amanda has a brilliant way of sharing what true embodied integrity looks like in today's digital landscape and truly leads by example."

—Sahara Rose, bestselling author and host of *Highest Self Podcast*

"*Followed* is the roadmap for social media success and personal fulfillment. If I had *Followed* when I started creating content, I would have made more money, saved years of stress, and found my mission as a creator years earlier."

—Lewis Howes, *New York Times* bestselling author of *The School of Greatness* and host of *The School of Greatness Podcast*

"If you are a coach or therapist, the same trauma that made you want to help others may now be holding you back from being successful online. It's been a joy for me as Amanda's coach to watch her create massive impact and success online while navigating the traumas resurfacing in her business with grace and grit. *Followed* is her playbook for how you can do the same."

—Mastin Kipp, trauma-informed coaching pioneer and author of *Claim Your Power*

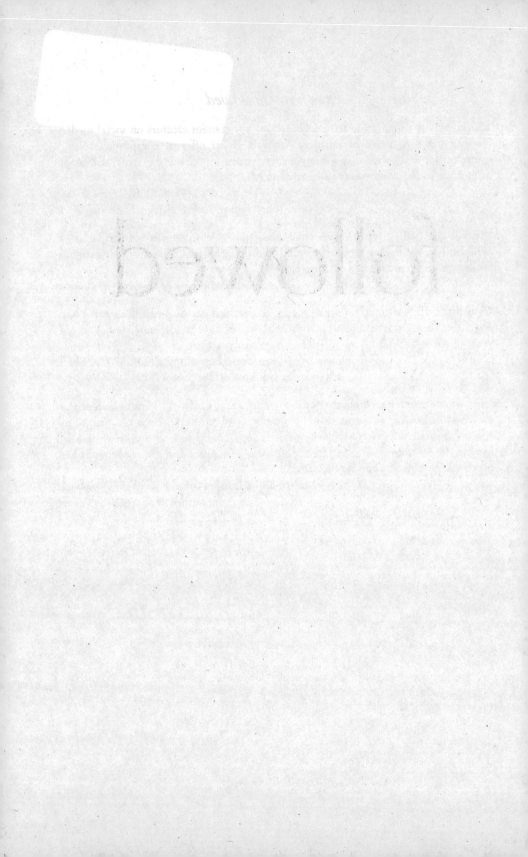

followed

followed

The Content Creator's Guide to Being Seen, Facing Judgment, and Building an Authentic Personal Brand

AMANDA BUCCI

BenBella Books, Inc.
Dallas, TX

This book is designed to provide accurate and authoritative information about entrepreneurship and content creators. Neither the author nor the publisher is engaged in rendering legal, accounting, or other professional services by publishing this book. If any such assistance is required, the services of a qualified financial professional should be sought. The author and publisher will not be responsible for any liability, loss, or risk incurred as a result of the use and application of any information contained in this book.

BenBella Books, Inc.
10440 N. Central Expressway
Suite 800
Dallas, TX 75231
benbellabooks.com
Send feedback to feedback@benbellabooks.com

BenBella is a federally registered trademark.

Printed in the United States of America
10 9 8 7 6 5 4 3 2 1

Library of Congress Control Number: 2022049286
ISBN 9781637742532 (hardcover)
ISBN 9781637742549 (electronic)

Editing by Claire Schulz, Rachel Phares, and Ruth Strother
Copyediting by Lydia Choi
Proofreading by Isabelle Rubio and Rebecca Maines
Indexing by WordCo.
Text design and composition by PerfecType, Nashville, TN
Cover design by Brigid Pearson
Printed by Lake Book Manufacturing

This book is dedicated to all of those who have followed along on my journey for years online. Thank you for bearing witness to my self-discovery journey. Thank you for seeing me. We've all come a long way.

contents

part III
Building an Authentic Personal Brand

a note from the author

***Followed* was written to support Content Creators in the journey of** having an online presence. The conversation around how being *followed* impacts the life trajectory of Content Creators is still a very novel topic, as we've only had social media for a few decades. It's time that we started talking about how to support Content Creators on a deeper level. It's my hope that this book sparks conversations in different communities across the internet about how to find more peace, confidence, and satisfaction throughout your journey as a Creator. My vision is for *Followed* to get passed around from one Creator friend to the next—and especially to the younger generations, who are already growing up with so many eyeballs on them and a bigger need to develop a strong sense of self than ever before.

I've been a Content Creator for almost ten years and have spent the majority of that time coaching thousands of other Creators to build awesome brands and businesses. But the one conversation I've found most important and impactful is how you, as a Creator, can remain true to yourself. Every single roadblock you face as a Content Creator—whether it's the fear of being seen, getting publicly called out, the pull to pivot your brand, or finding the courage to share your story—is a chance to grow. What you're about to dive into is a guide on how psychology, self-development, and emotional transformation intersect with social media, personal branding, and being *followed*.

The process of writing *Followed* helped me crystalize all the lessons I've learned on my own journey—from the identity crises, to getting publicly canceled and having my character called into question, to the social responsibility that comes with having influence. Looking back, social media has been the number-one place that's allowed me to really find myself, own my superpowers, and share them in a way that is so deeply satisfying and fulfilling in my life—and I'll be forever grateful for it. My favorite messages I get are from the people who say they've followed my journey for years and have loved witnessing my growth over time. They usually share a bit of how just observing as a follower for so long taught them so much, outside of the actual content and information I shared. To me, that's what being followed is all about—embodying your truth so much that people see it and are changed by just you existing.

Building an authentic online presence isn't just about marketing, being well liked, or following a formula to go viral—it's a journey of actively and courageously standing in your raw, gritty, authentic truth, even in the moments where you feel the watchful eye of people who tell you not to. It's about saying what you're called to say, expressing what you're called to express, and separating what you think you *should* do from what you're being moved and inspired to do. A calling is that thing that guides you to create, share, and post—and this book is here to help you soften the edges of every barrier that feels like it's in the way of you *boldly* and *bravely* following that calling.

Are you ready to answer that call?

introduction

Since the boom of social media in the mid-2000s, *millions* of people have started their own accounts in hopes of carving out their own little corner on the internet and benefiting from the opportunities of being a Content Creator. While platforms like YouTube, Instagram, Facebook, Twitter, TikTok, and Twitch have offered anyone the possibility to create success on their own terms, that same exposure has inherently given rise to judgment, criticism, and feedback.

> With great *visibility* comes great *vulnerability*.

For the first time in human history, anyone and everyone can amass a following without becoming a movie star, musician, or politician. People who might never have considered themselves artists are now calling themselves *Content Creators*. They're sharing their perspectives, expertise, resources, philosophies, humor, entertainment, art—and everything (and I mean *everything*) in between. In his landmark 2021 comedy special *Inside*, Bo Burnham brilliantly encapsulated living life online in his song "Welcome to the Internet," crooning, "Can I interest you in everything, all of the time?"

Content Creators believe they can make a difference in the world simply by being themselves. Your gifts live in your unique expression. The weirder you are, the stronger your presence. The more authentic you are, the greater the impact you will make—as that's what every single person on this planet craves to experience within themselves. Your voice can cause a ripple effect that transcends geographical boundaries. And then, a level of responsibility arises. You need to have integrity, adopt a growth mindset, show up and do your best—and do all of that to help you grow every single day while also benefiting your audience, too.

Followed is written and designed for you—the Content Creator—to find empowerment in putting yourself out there. It's about sharing your unique gifts to inspire, educate, or entertain others and moving on from those ideas, beliefs, and patterns that no longer serve you so you can be unencumbered as you move forward.

> This isn't just a business book, or a branding book, or a self-development book. It's all three.

Followed is not a how-to guide for influence. In these pages, you won't find a step-by-step strategy for growing a social media audience; however, by implementing what you read, you'll attract a following who will feel inspired by what you create and be compelled to share it. This isn't a book that you read once and place on the shelf; it's a resource you can return to over and over, picking it back up whenever it calls to you. There's a chapter relevant for every experience—regardless of whether you're just starting out or you've been publishing your thoughts and ideas since the days of LiveJournal and quoting emo lyrics in your AIM away message. There are also plenty of exercises throughout to help you integrate the deeper concepts. Think of the book as a supportive ally, often revealing new wisdom that only makes sense as you have new experiences, transition your business, switch platforms, or undergo a change in your life that prompts a change in your content. *Followed* is designed to help guide you in using your artistic energy to create content that serves your audience and connect you to your authentic self—a journey that never ends (in the best way possible!). It will be a lifetime of rewarding experiences, valuable lessons, and beautiful growth, in fact. How exciting!

In these pages, you'll read perspective shift after perspective shift, shattering you with newfound truths that'll stop you in your tracks and activate you to realize your potential and bigness. Whether it's your path to building a smaller, targeted audience who will help you build a six-figure coaching business or building an audience of multimillions who will follow you with each pivot you make—this book will help you:

- Find your unique niche on your social media platform without feeling *imprisoned by your online persona*
- Experience a *decrease in emotional intensity* in response to negative *judgments* and *opinions* of other people
- Familiarize yourself with *tools* to navigate emotional ups and downs, anxiety, uncertainty, rejection, judgment, and overwhelm related to your *social media growth journey*
- Stop comparing yourself to others and *define success* on your own terms
- Find your *community of people* who are dying for more of the exact flavor you provide
- Create content that lands, at your own pace, in a way that aligns with you, free from the *immense pressure* to constantly keep up with other Creators
- Minimize *disruptions* to your well-being as a result of the stresses of social media
- Experience more *strength and self-trust* to say yes to opportunities that'll provide you with more exposure, visibility, and growth

Being followed can and will bring about stressful and often scary internal experiences related to being seen, facing judgment, and receiving criticism. You'll start to look at your relationships with money, survival, success, achievement, and comparison, too. *Followed* will walk you through the process of seeing how your own self-protection mechanisms may be showing up in your relationship with social media and will show you how to begin transforming. The best recommendation I have for any Content Creator is to begin understanding how you can protect your peace and equip yourself with the tools to effectively navigate the inevitable ups and downs in your journey.

Followed will guide you through how to set and enforce boundaries, navigate PR nightmares, and manage conflict with others online—even if it sometimes means telling someone to *fuck off*, and then blocking them. You'll learn the practical strategies to protect your mental health, produce your best work, and work through the blocks that hold so many of us back from expressing ourselves authentically online.

Followed will validate your experience, challenge your beliefs, and extract the juicy, beneficial lessons available to you within your social media growth journey. Because when you discover what "being you" really looks like, your impact will be felt—just by *existing*.

HANDLE WITH CARE

With the addition of this new world, this new plane of existence, this new space with its own very particular texture—we've all gotta find our way to navigate it. There is no more "real world." As much as social media is a "version" of reality and not reality in its fullness, so too is the "real world." What we do online has a very direct and very real impact on what happens in the "real world," and vice versa. Starting a social media account should notify you with a pop-up warning label: *handle with care*. That's what this book is. Not only is it a manual for Content Creators to minimize the potential for pitfalls and optimize for opportunity—it's also a personal-development tool to support your growth as you walk along this path. Your entire humanity is considered in this book: from your earliest childhood experiences to how you feel when a follower judges you for existing in a way they disagree with. Whatever you feel and experience in this space is an opportunity for you to see yourself more fully, gather new lessons, and level up in life. Stay with me for the rest of this book, and I guarantee your entire world will start to change—one piece of content at a time.

part one
part one
part one
part one

The Foundations of Becoming an Authentic Content Creator

one

What Does It Mean to Be "Followed"?

I remember the day I posed for my first mirror selfie in the bathroom of my college dorm. I wore a bright-pink sports bra and white booty shorts, and I popped my hip out and smiled as I saw my baby abs peek through. The camera quality wouldn't hold up to today's standards, and yet that moment feels high-definition in my memory. But in the process of posting the photo, I noticed that I felt proud of myself, excited to share my progress and be witnessed by . . . well, anyone. I wanted to be *followed*. People were going to follow me and watch as I did life. Simultaneously, I felt both exhilarated and apprehensive at that thought. As many other Content Creators do, I asked myself the underlying question, "Should I be myself or the person other people want me to be?" Being *followed* by others online compels each of us to reflect on these intimidating questions:

- Who is the type of person that will want to follow me?
- What do I have to say?
- What do I bring to the table that doesn't already exist?
- Does it even matter?
- Who am I, anyway?

Very early on in life, most people learn and start to believe a version of the message: *don't be yourself too loudly.* Whether it's staying the course and getting a "respectable job," being told to stop crying, or getting condemned for making a mistake—we all have those forces in our lives that remind us to stay small inside the boxes we're "supposed" to stay in. Whenever we learned not to be ourselves too loudly, we also developed patterns of self-suppression, self-protection, and smallness by organizing ourselves into neat boxes of anything deemed "acceptable" and staying far away from the "unacceptable."

Social media is a place that comes with its own preconceived notions of needing to fit in and be well liked to succeed. What do you need to do to get someone to follow you? How can you create content that adds enough value to other people's lives to receive the benefits and gain you're creating for? Whenever you join a new platform and start an account, you bring along all of your own beliefs about who you are in the world and what you have to do in order to be liked, followed, and accepted. Whether you're a holistic-health expert who suffers from an autoimmune disease, a relationship coach who is currently amidst a divorce, or a meme account who simply feels like an imposter behind the screen, you'll find that your social media reality is a mirror image of your current subconscious narratives, projected onto your phone screen—confronting you, hundreds of times a day.

The weight of the eyes of others plays a major factor in how you choose to show up online. The question "What version of me can I share that will be presentable and acceptable to these people?" becomes the filter through which we make decisions about what we create, what we don't create, and the way in which we create—whether we consciously realize it or not. In conducting the market research for this book, I asked my audience what it was about social media that they really struggled with. One of the most popular complaints they had was how much they don't like the inauthentic, disconnected, fake energy they sometimes feel from Creators—and how that affects how they feel being in the social media environment as a result. Concomitantly, those who were Content Creators struggled with how they sometimes feel the need to be fake, inauthentic, or performative for their audiences. Let's talk about why this dynamic starts in the first place.

THE HUMAN DESIRE FOR VALIDATION

Validation is the act of reaffirming that someone's feelings, experience, or even existence is accepted, accurate, or okay to have. It's such a natural, human thing to seek validation from others, as receiving that feedback can help affirm we're on the right track, support us with managing our emotions, and make us feel accepted in relationships and in the world. It's an inevitable fact that Content Creators who are actively sharing content about themselves and their lives are also subconsciously checking to see if they'll be validated after they post. That feeling of checking to see how many comments, likes, shares, or saves you get is the same kind of communication of acceptance many people seek and need. How emotionally sensitive your content is (like coming out to your audience, sharing a vulnerable story, or announcing a life transition) will usually affect how much validation you're seeking.

In your journey and experience making content, validation seeking does mirror that human desire and need to be validated—but it can exacerbate or impact your emotional experience of whether or not you're receiving the kind of validation you might need to feel affirmed. Engagement is often used as a metric to measure how successful your account is, but Creators can often experience fluctuations in engagement as very personal activations of low self-confidence, self-doubt, and confusion about whether they're on the right track. The painful sting of not receiving that external validation from our content isn't something reserved only for those who are generally insecure—rather, it acts as a powerful yet subtle thread that can tug at any person, no matter how much work they've done on themselves. External validation has roots and themes in business (including subthemes of money, survival, success, and recognition), group belonging (connectedness and love), and self-esteem. Whether it's coming up with ideas, actually pressing "Post," engaging with comments, or dealing with the aftermath of a post—you might find yourself feeling like some of these themes stir up an emotional experience inside of you.

A great foundational practice for any Content Creator is becoming aware of your relationship to your likes, follower count, engagement rate, shares, subscribers, and downloads and noting how you feel about those numbers fluctuating in either direction. Have you ever felt that posting something that didn't feel authentic to you would get you more engagement—and did it anyway, even though it felt icky to you? Maybe you read somewhere that vulnerability was something Content Creators could show to foster trust with their audiences, so you conjured up a "vulnerable share" for the purpose of performing vulnerability for others—even though it didn't feel true to your heart. Perhaps you know that posing in a sexy way will get more likes, but you're in the process of shifting your brand to attract an audience of people who will hire you for your services—and you did the sexy poses anyway. Whatever it is, you've likely had at least one moment grappling with this inner conflict for yourself. Here's the deeper truth: although engagement can be a decent metric through which to affirm that what you're doing is something other people want, if you don't validate and affirm yourself first and foremost, you might find yourself in constant cycles of feeling disconnected from your social media.

Repeat this in your mind: *Regardless of who likes, comments, shares, or validates me—I will, first and foremost, always validate myself. There are so many skills to learn as a Content Creator, and I won't slip into the belief that I am the "problem" with my engagement.*

> "Authenticity requires a certain measure of vulnerability, transparency, and integrity."
>
> JANET LOUISE STEPHENSON

SOCIETAL AND INDUSTRY EXPECTATIONS

"Stay in your lane."

"Stick to your main content."

"I didn't sign up for this."

Criticisms like these abound in the comments sections of Content Creators bold enough to color outside the lines and share other parts of themselves on their platforms. This leaves many Creators feeling hesitant to share themselves, internalizing their authentic thoughts, opinions, and experiences as things to be ashamed of. Rather than accepting you as you are, many followers would prefer to keep their idea of you in a neat little box that suits their idea of who you are in their minds. This can feel similar to having a disapproving family and hiding your tattoos, sexuality or gender identity, or personality. The popular Amazon Prime series *The Marvelous Mrs. Maisel* follows the story of the titular character, a fictional Jewish comic in 1950's New York who shoulders the disapproval of her family as she spends evenings schlepping from their posh Upper West Side apartment down to Greenwich Village to perform at seedy comedy clubs in pursuit of her dream. Abuela Madrigal from the Disney movie *Encanto* alienated her granddaughter Mirabel to present a picture of a perfect family to the outside world, leaving Mirabel to feel like her ordinary existence wasn't enough. Both of these characters had to push back against their families and communities to just exist naturally as they are.

followed

Whether you're a mom who doesn't want to breastfeed, a person who doesn't fit into standards of gender identity and expression, a doctor who wears bikinis and cute outfits online, or an OnlyFans Creator sharing about your spirituality—you're a trailblazer breaking those societal norms.

Past Pain and Self-Protection Patterns

Unresolved mental and emotional trauma, pain from the past, and the subconscious patterns that formed as a result of these will often become activated through the experience of creating content. Trauma—which is discussed in chapter six—is an experience that overwhelms our systems and leaves a lasting impact in how we experience the world. On social media, Creators will often face situations in which their subconscious patterns will protect them from reexperiencing pain but might manifest in things like perfectionism, lack of boundaries, people-pleasing, anxiety, codependency, and more. This book is not to be taken as medical- or mental-health advice but will outline various ways to rewire some of those patterns in order to support you in experiencing more peacefulness and content in your social media experience.

THE VULNERABILITY OF VISIBILITY

For so long, we've seen tabloid magazines and celebrity gossip show us what it's like to have millions of eyeballs on you, watching you like a hawk, dissecting your every move—and even making up lies about someone for greed and profit. Even though most people have generally placed themselves in the observer position (rather than in the shoes of the celebrity), social media has changed that completely. More people than ever have now gained the opportunity to amass their very own followers, observers, and critics. And now, we have Reddit threads, comment sections, dedicated haters, and daily opportunities to be misconstrued, judged, and condemned for really anything—as simple as someone not liking the sound of your voice. If you're a Creator, you're more aware than ever of what the potential consequences of being seen, developing an audience, and developing a sense of fame feel like—even if it's just in some small corner of the internet. Choosing content creation means choosing to become more confident and comfortable with yourself and grounded in your authentic truth—because this environment will lead you to see that it's the only option. Each challenge is a mirror for our own internal growth, and each post is an opportunity to stay true to ourselves.

COURTING AUTHENTICITY, ONE POST AT A TIME

Much of the larger conversation about social media seems to focus on its potential for problems, how it's the source of a million never-ending ills. It can quite simply seem like a "bad" place, to be avoided at all costs—a catch-22 of spending as much time on it as possible to succeed, but not so much that it destroys your brain and self-confidence. How disempowering is it to be told that you'll always need to deal with the stresses and pressures of social media, with it being this bothersome and necessary evil, if you want success? That there's nothing you can do but expect to deal with it if you want to be a Content Creator?

Right here, right now—we're going to write a new narrative, together.

Social media is not without its downsides, but we must also acknowledge its potential for helping Creators break through the barriers holding them back from their authentic creative expression. When a Content Creator chooses to put themselves in the social media game, their gifts ripple out onto their audiences and communities. They teach, guide, entertain, and bring joy, perspective, and permission to hundreds, thousands, or even millions of people every single day. The momentum of progressive growth is like a snowball that continues to build and build. That energy is palpable and powerful. Every year, Content Creators push the edges of the world, show more people what's possible, and share more wisdom and knowledge—and the world grows and expands at an alarmingly rapid rate. As a Content Creator, you are a part of the revolution.

On a personal level, choosing to be a Content Creator will become one of the biggest accelerators for your personal growth that you'll ever experience. If you work on examining your relationship to yourself and social media, disconnecting from rigid societal programming, and always seeking the path to the most authenticity in your Creator journey—well, there's a whole world of freedom on the other side. In this world, your social media persona doesn't feel like a fake front or a persona you have to pretend to be to keep it going—it just feels like . . . you. In doing this, you'll break free from the imaginary boxes that were always too small for you anyway.

And in such a world, people will say, "Yep, I want more of that. I want to be a part of that. How can I keep getting the feeling I get from being in your community?" Not only that, but you'll feel unbothered when someone says, "Nope, you're not for me" because repelling those who aren't your people is simply a fantastic filter. This is the meta shift that's happening in the social media sphere, giving creators across the world greater permission to be exactly who they are.

Being *followed* is an experience that will challenge you to become more comfortable and confident in yourself than ever before. Through the battles you'll face with shattering societal expectations, challenging industry standards, and facing your own internal narratives of self-doubt—you'll find that being *followed* is one of the most beneficial paths for your personal expansion.

two

Embodying Your Inner Content Creator

In the earlier days of social media, we'd see formulaic models of what a "fitness influencer" account looked like, or a "spiritual account," or a "meme account." The general success strategy taught was to follow those models of success and do the same things other people did, and in doing so, you could build an audience. But what happened as the subsequent result was a news feed where every Creator started looking alike, talking alike, and repeating the same things. Industries felt saturated and robotic. Consumers didn't want to keep seeing the same carbon copies of Creators, and Creators didn't want to feel like another carbon copy. Inevitably, Creators like you and I decided we needed to become more innovative with how we shared ourselves online—so we could feel like *us*, not like another one of everyone else. In that exploration of uncharted territories, we're doing more of what's unexpected and daring, feeling absolutely on fire from what that brings out within us.

How can you take what's already being done and upgrade it in your own way—just a little bit? Can you take a current trend and give it your own twist? How can you write about a topic that's been covered thousands of times and present it with your unique perspective? Embodying your inner Content Creator is really the journey of discovering your untapped potential and finding your authentic voice—and each piece of content you publish can bring more clarity and confidence.

PUT THE *CREATIVITY* BACK INTO CONTENT CREATION

You may feel as if you need to fit a certain mold to be successful on social media, but Content Creators don't usually fit into perfectly defined boxes. You are multidimensional and dynamic, filled with unlimited potential and endless possibilities. You know—deep down—there *must* be a way in which you can be fully yourself and create success on this platform. There has to be. And, of course, you'll always figure it out.

From time to time, you may fall into the trap of performing the persona others expect of you. You may find it simpler to play it safe, not be too polarizing, and minimize the stress and difficulty of your experience that way—which is perfect, too. You aren't obligated to share everything or try to make every everyone happy, even if people expect you to cater to them. Remember, you get to design your account 100 percent your way, with every right to keep parts of yourself private and protected.

But in those moments when you *do* share a part of yourself that you haven't before and you allow yourself to be seen, hopefully you can recognize how impactful it is when you are just . . . you. Pure, unadulterated, and seen. You might just come to accept that perhaps the parts of yourself that you've been insecure about, questioned, judged, or hidden are *nothing* to be ashamed of. People who resonate in even the slightest way will find you, regardless of any algorithm. And all of a sudden, opportunities will arise. People will want to hear more. You may get offered brand deals, start your own business, or find your personal tribe of followers and friends. And better than that? You'll have an intrinsic connection to who you are, with an audience that's a resounding *fuck yes* to all that you stand for, and opportunities will become available to you as a result.

But it's not all about "just being yourself." Far from it. You know better than anyone that being a Content Creator isn't some easy, silly hobby. It requires time, effort, energy, and consistent hard work to become successful. Strategizing, ideating, filming, writing, editing, producing, posting, and engaging online on a semi-daily basis is a full-time job.

When I was twenty-two years old, I learned how to work a professional camera, edit thirty-minute-long videos, download copyright-free music, match its beat to my footage, research hashtags, and more . . . all in under six months. Content Creators are resourceful in that way.

Here are some actions you may find yourself doing as a Content Creator:

- Keeping up with the latest trends and strategies
- Studying different hooks for videos or captions
- Taking photos, filming videos, and editing to make them engaging for each platform
- Writing copy for captions or long-form content
- Designing graphics, researching color psychology, and curating font pairings
- Brainstorming ideas for content pieces
- Developing a strategy for your content to lead to an ideal outcome
- Seeking knowledge and skills to enhance engagement growth
- Experimenting and playing around with different technologies, techniques, and approaches to creating content
- Analyzing data and interpreting it to make decisions accordingly

followed

- Engaging with people in messages and private conversations
- Organizing your content in some outside system or software
- Posting content in different places, editing it to fit the platform
- Hiring contractors to support you in different stages of content creation and production

CONSISTENCY: THE ULTIMATE TEACHER

Content Creators all have different goals, niches, styles, and focuses—but you'll start off as an individual, creating your own short- and long-form media for whoever wants to hear it. *What you share matters to you*. It's that simple. You may not be the most talented, the most stylish, the most popular, or the loudest—but you're learning to trust that what you have to say *will* make an impact and add value to someone out there. And the more consistently you show up and do that? People will come. Yes, becoming a highly skilled Creator and working with the platforms' functionalities are a component to that growth—but the simple act of posting teaches you multiple invaluable lessons that you couldn't learn by thinking. Doing is the ultimate teacher.

THINKING IN CONTENT AND MINIMIZING OVERWHELM

"Thinking in content ideas" is a skill Content Creators develop when they immerse themselves in social media. *Anything* can be content—so you might begin viewing your life, the world, and your experiences as opportunities to create more content. As you get better at navigating the flow between living your life and turning it over into content, you'll come to find (if you haven't already) what a fantastic opportunity it is for both you and your audience to learn and grow in real time. In the early stages of being a Creator, you may wonder how you'll ever come up with ideas consistently. But over time, all you'll be able to think will be "I could use that as a TikTok, a caption, an email, a podcast!"

Here are some questions to ask when sourcing content ideas from your daily life:

- How can I take what's happened to me and relate it back to what I do or the content I teach regularly?
- How can I put what's in my brain on top of this trend or format?
- How can I share this random experience in a unique or creative way?

Because of this, content creation can become a source of overwhelm. If anything and everything could become content, what's to stop yourself from thinking about it 24/7? Most Content Creators will—in at least one point in their career—struggle with the pressure to keep up with creating content and for content to look perfect and polished, and they'll feel the cycles of creativity slumps. If you're a business owner, it might feel like you need to make content to keep getting in front of your potential customers. If you're an influencer, you might feel pressure to include your audience in your life by making content everywhere you go.

This is where developing your own systems, agreements, and protocols for how you navigate your content-creation journey will become important. Because there's a constant, niggling reminder that you could—at any point—be making *more* content than you already are, it's up to you to set boundaries, accept ebbs and flows, and minimize stress and pressure for yourself.

HAVING A UNIQUE PERSPECTIVE

The confident Content Creator believes they *deserve* to be online and that what they have to say and share holds value. If you're still learning this lesson, struggling with imposter syndrome, or worrying that what you have to say doesn't matter—that's okay, too. Most Creators struggle with this in the beginning. But consider this: billions of women have been pregnant and had babies. Many of those women have shared their own journey through pregnancy and into motherhood. All of the basic information about that process is probably out there at this point. But there are thousands of people in one woman's audience who are not at the place in their life to be ready to receive content about pregnancy until that particular Creator begins sharing her journey. That one Creator can help her audience, a very specific group of people, through the learning process of pregnancy with her specific perspective. This doesn't mean those people couldn't have found that information elsewhere, but it does mean they wanted to hear it from *her*.

Having a perspective is the one thing you need as a Content Creator. You don't have to be the best, smartest, funniest, or the most put together. You just have to find a way to continuously tap into what feels most authentically *you*. Living the version of you that you actually are—moment to moment—is trusting the natural unfolding of what you want to create, following those urges of inspiration that pop up along the way, and using your discernment when your process begins to feel obligatory or forced.

Here are some authenticity questions to ask yourself:

- What does it feel like when I'm "performing" for my audience?
- What does it feel like when I'm doing what feels most like me online?
- What does my tone of voice sound like when I'm relaxed?
- How is the camera positioned, graphics written, or art displayed?
- What stories am I buying into that have led me to believe I cannot be myself?

ADOPTING THE IDENTITY OF A CONTENT CREATOR

Adopting the identity of a Content Creator may feel a little clunky at first. You might not be sure if this is actually you. You may have judgments about Content Creators as a whole or feel concerned that you'll be perceived as a certain type of Content Creator that you don't necessarily like. You might, for example, think Creators are superficial or frivolous, or perhaps not see their role as a real pursuit worth your time and energy. This is an opportunity to acknowledge any judgments you're holding about Content Creators and begin examining and interrogating them.

- What is this belief showing me about what I don't want?
- Is it possible for me to be a Content Creator without being like "that"?
- What do I feel about "that"?
- Does holding on to this judgment serve me?

Perhaps you're scared to piss people off because you've been pissed off before. Great! Can you acknowledge that the mere act of existing will piss some people off, that you cannot avoid offending everybody, and that you'll learn to adopt various perspectives of compassionate creation along the way? Perfect.

Take a moment to let that land.

Realize that you get to form your own version of the Content Creator identity. It is your personal expression and experience of it for you to shape your sense of identity around. You are aligning to a "higher," more evolved, integrated, and experienced version of yourself—not anyone else. There is no perfect avatar, guru, or model for this, except the one inside of you who is making these platforms your own.

USING CONTENT CREATION TO ACCESS YOUR AUTHENTIC CREATIVE EXPRESSION

Every Creator has their own reasons for making content. Some are in it for business purposes and use social media as a means to an end. Some love having a place to express their talents and entertain people, while others are out to educate the masses and support people in growth. Regardless of your reason, if you make any kind of content, it requires a connection to your own creativity.

Creativity is a force of nature that is very close to our most natural state—receptive, imaginative, and experimental. It provides you with those pangs of inspiration, ideas, and enthusiasm. Whether it's an email, a painting, or an entire business—creativity flows *through* you.

Think of the last time you felt creative. You were likely lit up by an idea—and lost track of time as you flowed with the energy of that idea. You allowed that force to move through your body and let it take the lead until you created something beautiful.

> "People frequently believe the creative life is grounded in fantasy. The more difficult truth is that creativity is grounded in reality, in the particular, the focused, the well observed or specifically imagined."
>
> JULIA CAMERON, *THE ARTIST'S WAY*

Creativity is following the nudges of desire that lead you to create. We cannot control creativity or force it to show up on demand. We can only open our hearts, take care of ourselves, and clear our minds from distraction in order to give it the opportunity to land at our doorstep.

As a Content Creator, you interact with creativity every single day. Even if you aren't posting every day, creativity is knocking at your door with potential content ideas for your platform. The quiet voice that consistently pipes up with *What will I create today?* may feel like a nuisance at times, but what if it was creativity (your best friend!), guiding you back to your platform to share . . . yourself? What if, when you feel stuck, plateaued, or disconnected, you viewed that as a symptom of being disconnected from your creative self and a reminder to reconnect to the imaginative, experimental part of you?

But it's not always that easy—let's discuss why that may be.

The Wounded Creator

Most children are encouraged to live and express themselves creatively through games, toys, painting, singing, dancing, and playing instruments. But when many children enter adolescence—especially in the Western world—they are taught that their natural, embodied creative expression is less valuable. And most of the time, by adulthood, it's firmly squashed down.

"Artists don't make any money!" says the parent who wants their child to be financially successful.

"Dancing is fruity!" says the homophobic father devaluing the free, fluid expression in his son.

"Stop being silly and get serious about life!" says the teacher to the student who has a wild imagination, is probably neurodivergent, and struggles to focus in class.

"This art is mediocre," says society to the child who simply enjoys painting for themself. They're told it's a waste of time unless they become a wildly skilled and masterful artist.

Many children have had their creativity suppressed by outside forces at some point in their lives. I distinctly remember enjoying singing in the middle-school choir so much that I started taking solo singing lessons once a week. I then competed in a singing competition, where I performed in front of four judges. I ended up getting Bs and Cs for my performance. As much as this grading system is useful to highlight those who will eventually become the masters, a class above the mediocre, that moment left a stain on my identity forever. From then on, I believed I couldn't be creative *unless* I was very good at it. So I stopped singing and didn't pursue any creative passions for another ten years.

This is the experience of the *wounded Creator* many of us have living inside of us.

> "No matter what your age or your life path, whether making art is your career or your hobby or your dream, it is not too late or too egotistical or too selfish or too silly to work on your creativity."
>
> JULIA CAMERON, *THE ARTIST'S WAY*

As an adult and Content Creator, you have the special opportunity to unlearn those belief systems and rebuild new ones as you explore your own authentic self through your content-creation processes. You may find yourself judging how "good" your content is or waiting to be validated by your audience to tell you how good it is. Pay close attention to the signs of perfectionism, not-enoughness, and the avoidance of experimenting.

BUILDING A RELATIONSHIP WITH YOUR CREATIVITY

Being in a relationship with your own creativity helps you break past barriers of stuckness in your journey as a Content Creator—because no amount of strategy can make up for not feeling inspired. To begin building this relationship, start by fiercely guarding your creative time. If you give creativity the energy, attention, and focus it deserves, you'll be surprised as to what can unfold and the ideas you can have. To me, it feels like my inner genius is *always* waiting to come out—all I have to do is quieten the external noise and give it the space to come through.

Next, take the pressure off of yourself to "perform" at any particular cadence, frequency, or quality. Sure, there are plenty of rules and ideals for how you can "best" grow your audience—but trying to force your creativity when it's just not there is not useful. In fact, many Content Creators I know report that the content that gets produced out of force just doesn't land with their audiences the same way their inspired content that has percolated fully and is then intentionally curated does.

Although creativity and the mystery of its unpredictable, nonlinear nature cannot be controlled, there are practices you can engage in to increase its chances of arrival and decrease its chances of hiding. Best-selling author of *Big Magic* Elizabeth Gilbert calls this "creative living," or living a life that prioritizes creative expression.

Gilbert claims that creative living isn't just doing things to come up with more ideas but rather finding ways to incite *awe, wonder, curiosity, intrigue, emotion, passion,* and the *unknown*. This can be done through new experiences, socializing, spirituality, being in nature, writing, painting, singing, sculpting, moving, walking, business, and reading—anything that will pull you out of the monotony and cyclical nature of day-to-day life and place you into something . . . different. So rather than simply sitting and wondering,

followed

"What content should I create today?" ask the question alongside adopting the principle of creative living.

> "The older I get, the less impressed I become with originality. These days, I'm far more moved by authenticity. Attempts at originality can often feel forced and precious, but authenticity has quiet resonance that never fails to stir me."
>
> ELIZABETH GILBERT, *BIG MAGIC*

FOCUS YOUR ATTENTION AND DIRECTION

No one will follow you for a few irrelevant TikToks, one article on your website, an email list you contact sporadically, or Instagram posts that are reposted and filled with regurgitated content from other Creators. As much as social media is a free space within which to do whatever you choose, structure, direction, and focus will help you make the best use of your time online. To channel your creativity, focus on a few core activities:

1. **Master one or two platforms.** Understand how each of them work, study different content structures that are working for other Creators in your niche, and experiment every single day with your unique perspective. Give yourself the best chances for success by following the conventions of each platform.
2. **Slow down to speed up.** Creating consistently *and* successfully requires you to have a solid direction, strategy, and system in place

to begin picking up the speed and frequency of production with time. Slow down, really think about what you want to say and how you want to present it, and gather helpful data from these initial experiments before you go full force.

3. **Refine your content-creation style, message, and purpose.** A brand that has people wanting to come back for more is organized around a central purpose, style, message, or movement. Spend some time thinking about what your core focus is for your platform.
4. **Organize your creative space with systems you can follow.** For some people, that's batching content in a single day and organizing it with a project-management system. For others, it's keeping all your ideas in one place (like the notes section of your phone, or apps like Notion and AirTable) and executing them when you feel inspired. Either way, find a way to structure your ideas so they don't feel like they're floating around in your mind without an anchor.
5. **Use your platform to stay accountable.** If you say you're going to create one TikTok a day for thirty days, tell your audience and let them know what kind of content they can expect from you. True accountability works when other people are genuinely reliant on you to follow through, rather than when someone taps you on the shoulder and asks, "Hey, did ya do that thing you said you were gonna do?"
6. **Know where you're sending people after they see your content.** For many, social media content creation is not the be-all and end-all when it comes to making money online. Affiliate partnerships, brand deals, and businesses are all ways to leverage your audience to create various revenue streams for yourself. If you're not feeling clear on how your content links directly to your offers, you may find yourself demotivated to create content. If this is true, ask yourself: How do I add value to my audience in a way that leads them to want to invest more into my products or services? What content may they want or need to see related to what I sell? If you are unsure, we'll be covering how to monetize your content in a later chapter.

followed

WAYS TO ENHANCE YOUR CREATIVITY

Becoming stuck and feeling resistant to creating content is a completely common and natural experience that every Content Creator goes through at some point in their journey. As much as I absolutely adore creating content on social media and have for the last near-decade, it's still something that requires a lot of thoughtfulness, intentionality, time, and energy. Even when you have a clear plan for what you're going to create and how you'll create it, producing content is still a multistep process including ideation, writing/recording, editing, posting, repurposing, and engagement. Free-flowing, easy, excited, and inspired energy is one of the main ways we can stay connected to and consistent with our content-creation process, even when it starts to feel like a job. After years of my own content creation every single day, I definitely had to come to terms with the fact that I had to be an active participant in harnessing that creative energy for content creation on a regular basis. Here are some effective and energizing ways to keep creativity high.

Space

Creativity thrives when you carve out room (in your life, in your calendar, in your awareness) for inspiration. This could look like spending those early-morning hours when no one is awake writing or filming, or spending time on the weekend doing absolutely nothing and allowing the thinking mind to take some time off. This will allow that more intuitive, introspective part of you to come alive and be fully open to receiving ideas, focusing on your creative project, and innovating to bring fresh perspectives into existence.

Space can also mean assessing and rearranging your environment—that is, your physical space (your home, your office) and your mind to better elicit creativity. If you're in a cramped studio apartment with a bunch of roommates or working in an overcrowded café, it might not be as productive as having your own studio or joining a coworking space. You may, however, thrive being around loads of people and vibe off their energy, so working in a quiet but buzzing coffee shop may be your jam.

Structure

Without structure, you may feel disconnected and unmotivated to create content. Think of it in terms of the different elements: *air*, *earth*, *fire*, and *water*. Creativity has a very *airy* texture. Think about how imaginative space or clouds make you feel. Without the element of *earth* to ground those ideas, they'll just kind of . . . float by. Without the element of *fire*, they'll feel a little dull and lack passion, excitement, or emotionality. Structure gives your ideas the containment they need to thrive, just as *water* needs a vessel or some sort of structure to take shape, be held, and become useful. So if you find yourself lost, you may be missing:

- Clear direction and priorities
- An overall plan and strategy
- An easy-to-follow, repeatable system
- Milestones and accountability

Hiring an online coach, taking a class from an expert, or seeking information from books or podcasts can be ways to learn more about how to implement structure into your life. If you're looking for an accessible space to learn more about structuring your workflow and business as a Content Creator, you can head to the various articles and courses website—www.amandabucci.com—to learn more about building an online business.

Purpose

Similar to incorporating structure, creating from a place of feeling connected to a deeper purpose enhances that internal drive and motivation to continue when work feels a little stagnant, monotonous, or overwhelming. You could interpret "purpose" in the more esoteric sense of feeling like you're "living your purpose" or "knowing what you're here on Earth to do." But that doesn't work for everybody, nor is it required to feel purposeful! Purpose could simply mean you know *why* you're doing something, *what* you're getting out of it, and *how* it supports you in your life. Is content creation helping you become a better writer? Is it fun, and is fun an important value for you? Simple as that!

Emotional Safety and Regulation

Your nervous system, internal stress responses, and feelings of safety in the body are major factors that affect creativity. It's not necessary to have a perfectly regulated nervous system to be creative—hell, many artists and creatives create from the depths of pain, sadness, or anger. And yet: sharing your creative ideas is *inherently vulnerable*—and your lived experience, traumas, or wounds may prevent you from feeling regulated enough to do that. If you've struggled to be creative or consistent due to your mental health, trauma, or wounding, know that it completely makes sense. Search for emotional-regulation tools online, seek out support groups, go to therapy, or find other avenues that'll allow you to take care of your mental and emotional health.

Easy Wins and Validation

There's often a flood of dopamine and validation that hits when your post pops off, goes viral, or gets a lot of shares—and guess what? That's perfectly okay. Little reminders that what you're doing is reaching, impacting, and influencing people are highly motivating and can make you feel alive. Of course, it's important to acknowledge that trying to create "just for the likes" isn't sustainable. However, sometimes when you're working on longer-term creative projects where momentum can wane, having those little hits on the side can give you the juice to keep going.

Audience Engagement and Feedback

Connecting with your audience or community is a powerful way to activate creativity! There's nothing like direct feedback about your content to motivate you to continue creating, expanding, and developing. When someone comments on a post or sends you a private message, it can spark a whole new angle or point of view you hadn't considered. Perhaps you'll learn something new or become inspired to create a new offering in an area that you didn't even realize was a topic of interest or concern.

Novelty and Innovation

Whether it's a photo shoot, a brand relaunch, or trying a new social platform, bringing fresh energy and innovation to your process can spark so much creativity. Novelty or newness is like a pattern interruption that can jolt you out of the mundane and into the magical. Repetition and dedicated consistency are what allow your ideas to come to life in tangible form, but novelty and newness are where those ideas can arise in the first place. Creativity is all about movement—different, imaginative outside-of-the-box-ness. What's something you haven't done before? Could you come up with a way to do things even just a little bit differently than how you have been? Can you expand outside of your comfort zone and try going live instead of writing a post? Perhaps there's a different format, way of filming, style of background music, or modality of expression that's just waiting to be the vessel for your next idea. When stuck, *try different*.

Novelty can also give you the courage to try new ideas or step outside of your comfort zone in a way you wouldn't normally think to try. For example: when TikTok started gaining popularity, many Creators found themselves open to trying an entirely new platform with its own expression and thus accessed a version of themselves that was perhaps *more* free to express. Perhaps they were able to be funnier or express a different talent on that platform than with, say, Instagram or podcasting, where they'd developed a particular content-creation style that sometimes impeded their creativity.

Movement

Moving your body and connecting back to your own physical energy can also invoke creativity. It's easy to become stagnant or stuck in a rut or block, especially if you're working from home or sitting at a laptop all day. Consider adding in any kind of movement throughout your day that works for your schedule and abilities. This could look like adding in a walk, stretching, jumping up and down, EFT tapping, or any other kind of physical movement that feels good. If you're really stuck, try adding a *free-flowing* movement practice into your life. Activities like weight training or even dance classes can become very rigid, but turning some music on and allowing your body to move to the sound is more cyclical, body-based (getting out of the mind), and . . . free. One of my wonderful friends from Los Angeles, Julia Grace, is a dance therapist, and her ecstatic dance classes on the beach taught me how physically embodying cyclical, nonlinear movement in the body can help you break out of rigid, stuck energy. Any practice you can find like that to implement in your life—even in the comfort of your own home—can work wonders.

Inspiration

We all access inspiration from different places, so ask yourself: What is it that I get inspired by? Is it reading romance novels or historical biographies? Going to see a show on Broadway? Having epic travel experiences? Exploring different cultures? How about interacting with nature, psychedelics, or other Creators? Maybe you're inspired by movies, TV shows, contemporary art, or music. The list is endless and unique to every individual. Finding sources of inspiration that hit you at a sensory and emotional level will unlock deeper creativity.

Play and Enjoyment

Sometimes what your creativity really needs is for you to go offline, disconnect from social media, and have an absolute blast of a time. Hang out with friends, go to a party, play with some animals, or get out in nature! Having some good old fun mitigates stress, relaxes the body, and opens the mind. It helps you be in the world, experiencing all it has to offer—rather than living in your phone or computer, attempting to source creativity from those spaces. The experiences, stories, connections, conversations, and epiphanies you have offline will make for a richer expression of yourself online.

BLOCKERS OF CREATIVITY

If you're feeling stuck in your ability to conjure up and produce amazing content, there are plenty of places in your life that you can examine to see where you can free up blockages of creativity. Consider some of the below areas and whether or not you can adjust them to access that creative inspiration again.

Obligation

Obligation is the *killer* of creativity. Feeling like you *have* to complete a task on a certain timeline, in a certain way, and with a certain set of rules and parameters can be in conflict with the natural, organic unfolding of your creative flow. There are small, subtle ways we can buy into that sense of pressure and obligation—like the notion of needing to post every day to stay relevant—that we can let go of to free us from illusionary obligation. Sometimes it's necessary to post for business or brand deals, but you can create flexibility in other areas, like what time you need to post, how the post looks, or how much production you do to make the post the best it can possibly be. If you can begin releasing attachment to the "rules" and honoring your needs when you can, you'll most likely feel ease and flow come through. The goal is to not have your content creation feel like a chore.

Pressure

Pressure can be divided into two types: internal and external. Both can invoke a feeling of restriction, where it's close to impossible to flow and simply does not allow for creativity. External pressures can include deadlines, your audience, clients, and other people in your industry. Internal pressure comes from expectations we place on ourselves to fit a certain mold, be perceived a certain way, or not deviate from the "plan." Find small and large opportunities to release yourself from pressure and give yourself permission to be more easygoing with your content production.

Constant Content Creation

Creating the same type and style of content over and over can allow you to fall into a rut. It's exhausting to do the same thing every day. There's no space for new ideas to come through. When you're in that state, it can be very draining to try to be creative because you feel "blocked," and you might not even know what to try or what might help to create freedom. If this is you, take a break and do something else—anything different to get out of the monotony.

Consumption and Comparison

Consumption and comparison go hand in hand; it's a cycle where one feeds the other. It starts out with mindless scrolling and consuming other people's content. Before you know it, you're in "comparison mode" and looking around at what everyone else is creating, wondering whether your content is better or worse. It's playing a game of trying to be the best and doing what your mind believes will make you better. Originality and authentic creativity won't be birthed from this place. Try muting other accounts, turning your phone off, or taking breaks from social media to recenter yourself.

LET YOURSELF COME ALIVE

Remember: social media spaces are an open playground for your expression. They feel restricted for many reasons, especially when we're disconnected from our own inner magic.

Cut out the noise.

Go within.

Connect just you and your imagination.

How can you create room for the playful parts of you? The funny parts of you? The sexy parts of you? The philosophical parts of you? Do you have graphic-design formats you can pour yourself into? Fonts and colors that make you come alive? Photo-shoot outfits that allow you to be expressive? Ideas and messaging that flow from your fingertips like lightning? Or are you stuck in the small, restricted boxes with a sleepy, safe brand and content formats that feel limiting and small? Find more ways to *play* with your content and creativity—and watch more of your own authentic expression start to feel more comfortable coming out of its shell.

three

Are You Who They Think You Are?

In February of 2020, I finally felt ready to start writing my book. I attended a book-writing workshop led by Tucker Max, four-time *New York Times* best-selling author and founder of Scribe Media. Among other services, Scribe helps entrepreneurs write books. Not coincidentally, this is also the goal of Tucker's book *The Scribe Method*, which helps authors plan, structure, write, and publish their books.

The first exercise Tucker asked us to complete was to write two words on our name tag:

1. Our name
2. The word "Author"

An identity crisis befell most of the room, full of aspiring authors who were nervous and already riddled with imposter syndrome. Claiming to be an author only added to the doubts and pressures we were already feeling.

Author? Me? Not yet. I haven't written any books. Mostly just Instagram posts. Author?!

"As of today, you are officially an author. Take on that new identity. Without it, you'll never publish your book," Tucker said. I felt a gnawing emotion within me kick and scream, scrambling to resist this truth. I knew I'd have to eventually accept it, but in that moment, I felt far from ready.

No, but—wait. Wait wait wait. I'm not ready yet! I don't know anything! I don't even know if I can do this! What if my book sucks? Can I back out?

This inner push-pull phenomenon is a common human experience—feeling the inner conflict of wanting to do something scary while simultaneously wanting to back out. It's the battle of finding the inner strength to move forward on our big goals and dreams instead of staying cozy in our comfort zone. As a person creating content online, you may have had a similar knee-jerk reaction to claiming what it means for you to be a Content Creator.

THE BODY'S PHYSICAL AND EMOTIONAL BALANCING ACT

Scientifically speaking, our bodies have ancient operating systems that are designed to keep us safe from threats. This includes the limbic system, which regulates emotions, memories, and homeostasis, and the autonomic nervous system, which puts the body into hypoarousal and hyperarousal states as needed. Together, they make up our emotional nervous system—or our "internal alarm system." When we lived in hunter-and-gatherer times and needed to run from predators while hunting, our bodies developed the ability to become vigilant to our surroundings to prevent physical injury or death. The aim was to stay as safe as possible, always. Though we've evolved and (for the most part) are not in constant threat of physical survival, however, those systems haven't disappeared. These systems in our bodies function automatically as an instinct—which means that mental fortitude alone isn't enough to overcome repeated patterns of behavior, thought, and feelings when the whole system is designed to keep us safe.

On a psychological level, our identity, emotions, sense of self, and relational patterns come from our genetics, environment, upbringing, conditioning, lived experiences, and traumas. Every event in our life influences the way we view and experience the world—causing emotions, thoughts, and memories from the past to continually arise in present-moment situations. Being the intelligent instruments they are, our bodies have the instinctual drive to protect themselves, conserve energy, and avoid unsafe situations in the future. To make that happen, the body will anchor life experiences from childhood and early adulthood as "programs," or a physiological, automatic reaction in the body. For example, if you grew up extremely religious, you may have programs installed that say if you have sex outside of marriage, you're going to hell—which in turn install a program of shame around your sexualities and desires. Each program is like software within our system, and that software will unconsciously and automatically run in the background until we actively work on unraveling and reprogramming it.

You may have been loud and self-expressed but were told to be quiet, so you learned to be soft-spoken and agreeable, when you're actually fiery and strongly opinionated. You may have been artistic but were told it was better to be athletic, so you decided to train hard in the gym and receive validation for your body, abandoning your artistic side. You may have been quiet when you were younger, but your sibling got more attention and love for being more external and charismatic, so you contorted yourself into being more extroverted and now find yourself constantly burned out from never having proper alone time. These are just some examples of how our environments and conditioning shape who we are and how we show up in the world.

This kind of conditioning or programming can run so deep, you may not even be aware of it. Your protective functioning may be helping you to maintain homeostasis and psychological safety, but it's also likely operating under the belief that a part of who you naturally are is not the "right" way to be. In reality, who you naturally are has been okay all along—but your body has a deeply ingrained program that requires therapy, support, healing, and a way to safely expand those edges to release what no longer serves you.

Take a moment to apply this new understanding to your struggles on social media. Avoiding posting any content that may feel too polarizing or opinionated may be a form of self-protection. You might avoid showing up on video or in "bigger ways" and do what you can to blend in and not bring attention to yourself. Showcasing your intelligence, sharing certain aspects of yourself, or setting boundaries may be challenging for you because of your own internal programs. Those are our *patterns*—the internal systems of behavior, thinking, and feeling that when left unconscious can become the primary puppeteer of our lives.

> "Until you make the unconscious conscious, it will direct your life and you will call it fate."
>
> CARL JUNG

These masks and patterns do serve a purpose in our lives by keeping us as safe as possible for as long as possible. Take a moment to honor your body and system right now for being an incredibly brilliant vessel beyond your conscious understanding and keeping you safe. *Bravo, body.* Those patterns may feel annoying, frustrating, or limiting, but those patterns have been unconscious support systems, helping you out your entire life!

The good news about these patterns is that they can be *unlearned* to create a new reality altogether—a life that is more relaxed, authentically aligned, and supportive to your growth, evolution, and success. Millions of people are using social media to express themselves, create art, build brands, and make money. The opportunities are plentiful, and the lessons are abundant—but don't expect to grow a massive audience without coming in contact with your own patterns and programs. Rather, *expect* your patterns to show up when you're living on the edge of your comfort zone and arm yourself with the skills and knowledge of how your ego-based patterns function. It'll help you create *just* enough distance between your pattern and your potential to keep moving forward. Let's talk about how to do that.

SO, WHAT'S THE *EGO*?

The word "ego" is commonly used in describing someone who has a big self-concept, or who comes across as arrogant or conceited. The concept of the ego was first formulated by Sigmund Freud in 1923 and was later carried on by psychiatrist Heinz Hartmann.[1] In recent times, we've also been told through modern best-sellers that "ego is the enemy" and that in order to grow personally, we must rid ourselves of our ego. The narratives about what the ego is can often lead to misunderstanding it altogether, making it seem like it's better not to have an ego. But the truth is that every human has an ego because it's a part of the psyche.

Here's what you need to know about yourself and your ego: *your ego is an identity your brain has unconsciously built for yourself based on a combination of beliefs about who you are.* These beliefs have formed over the span of your entire life, influenced by every aspect of your environment—especially when you were a growing and developing child. There's no need to try and kill your ego or get rid of it. In fact, when you learn how to understand, listen to, and contend with your own ego (we'll discuss this in more detail through this chapter), it can actually lead to a greater sense of peace and self-acceptance.

One of the core ways to identify the voice of your ego is to notice the moments when you make yourself either inferior or superior to others—like those instances when you puff yourself up, saying, "But aren't I great? Better, even? Smarter? More than what these people believe I am?" One way the ego operates out of self-protection is to make you feel like you're better than, above, or superior to others. On the flip side, it will do the same in the negative context—making you feel smaller, inferior, or less than. Take a moment to remember the last time you felt either superior or inferior. This response is so common, it probably happened at some point today! The ego will make declarative statements about yourself like "I'm such a mess—who would ever want to follow me?" or "I'm way smarter than they are, so why do they have more followers than I do? Ugh." This inflation-and-deflation dance the ego moves through is an incredibly natural part of being human—but there are ways we can minimize or prevent the intensity of these thoughts and how they affect our subsequent actions. It's a part of you to *understand*, *embrace*, and *collaborate with*. In other words, the ego is actually more akin to a business partner than to a competitor.

How does the ego develop? The moment babies enter and explore the world after their very first breath, they immediately begin interpreting the world through every bit of sensory information they experience. But they don't think of the world the way an adult does, as they're still developing their cognitive abilities through different stages of development. Because babies cannot understand the world through an abstract, objective, or nuanced lens the way adults can, they interpret what's safe and what's unsafe, how to get their needs met, and what behaviors help them meet those needs through their senses. Everything that babies sense and experience is all they know about the world, so they learn what will help them survive in their environment, which includes physical needs like food, water, and shelter, along with emotional needs like love, support, and belonging. Depending on how life goes and what we experience at such a formative age, our brains will automatically anchor a lot of those experiences as important information—helping to form behavior patterns, our personality, and the structure of our ego. So much of this information lives in the subconscious, and until we start unearthing some of it, our ego will stick to its beliefs about who we are, what traits we have and don't have, what we're capable of and not capable of, and what we deserve and don't deserve.

This may be a tough concept to wrap your head around, as we're not used to thinking about ourselves as separate from a part of our minds. Typically, we live in a constant state of what's called "ego-identification," meaning that we heavily *identify* with our thoughts, feelings, behaviors, and beliefs. Without the awareness that the ego exists, we fully believe that we *are* those thoughts and feelings. Have you ever believed that you were an anxious person (rather than *a person experiencing anxiety*)? Or maybe you see yourself as an introverted person (rather than a *person experiencing overwhelm around other people*). That's ego. You may also be wondering how to discern between what's "you" and what's your ego. Keep reading, and let's go through some real-life situations where you can start bringing awareness to your own ego's patterns.

Social Media and the Ego

Social media is a place where we think about ourselves *far* more than we do outside of it—*especially* if you're a Content Creator. If you're making content regularly, there's a part of your brain that's constantly thinking about what to post next, how that post will be received, if it'll take you closer to your goals, and so on. The constant stream of creation puts a heavy emphasis on how often we think about who we are, what we have to say, and how we feel in relation to other people—which can be extremely activating for the ego. Think about it: How often do you compare yourself to others when you're scrolling on social media? How often do you unconsciously place yourself in a "better than, worse than" paradigm when on social media? Do you find yourself to be more self-conscious as a Content Creator while scrolling than when you aren't? If you don't know, try taking two days off of social media and see what happens. Being a Creator is like a constant open faucet for the ego, tempting Content Creators to share what they believe will get likes, comments, engagement, and validation. And if we don't work on fighting against that gushing outpour, it'll usurp our energy, empowerment, and self-confidence.

We all—even the most conscious and aware people—adopt some level of self-modulation on social media in an attempt to control the narrative of how we are perceived by the thousands of strangers who will never truly know us. Content Creators are just out there doing their best. No one is trying to be fake on purpose (unless, of course, they are). Most people are doing what they can to share authentically and be the most "them" they are currently capable of being. This is why social media is a vehicle for some of the biggest ego work you can do. We're constantly asking ourselves the questions:

- Who do I think I am?
- Who do they think I am?
- Who do I think they think I am?

As we continue throughout this book, I want you to practice observing the ways in which you modulate yourself on social media. The first step to calling back your confidence and self-empowerment is to become aware of when we lose or give away our power. In your observations, adopting the two thought frameworks below can be helpful:

1. **Neutral Observation.** Observe what you're thinking, feeling, and doing with neutrality. A neutral observation sounds like: "Oh, I see how I'm avoiding going live today because I'm scared of what people will say about how I look. *That's interesting.*" Resist the temptation to place a value on it (good, bad, right, or wrong).
2. **Compassion.** Hold yourself in a warm embrace of compassion and love. Compassion sounds like: "I forgive myself for judging myself. I can accept that these thought patterns are automatic habits and that it will take time and practice for me to change them." Moving forward is far more difficult when we're judging ourselves instead of accepting ourselves.

Practicing these two frameworks will feel challenging at first because you've likely done the opposite your entire life. Your brain will tell you that the pain of judging yourself is easier than the pain of transformation. Feeling better happens when we realize that we don't have to believe the thoughts our minds feed us, but we can become active participants in creating new thoughts and feelings. Deep down, we all just want to be accepted for who we are—and sharing content can feel like a vulnerable extension of that same deeper desire. When we finally decide to go ahead and show up online however the hell we please rather than how we believe we're expected to? It's liberating.

How to Spot Your Ego

The ego searches for labels, identities, feelings, and neat little boxes to attach itself to—also known as "ego-attachment." When attached to the beliefs our ego has about who we are, it's not uncommon to end up becoming mentally inflexible and feel stuck in those beliefs. Think back to a time when you felt like you were *so* right, *so* justified—and *no one* can tell you otherwise, even if the belief you're so tightly clinging to is less than helpful or supportive. Think about a moment when you felt like it was super important to tell someone off in your comments section or made that petty post about your ex—even when you knew it might stir up more issues and unnecessary strife. When we're attached to a position that's rooted in ego, it can be hard to consider that anyone else's perspective or opinion could also hold some truth. And alas, in times of conflict or disagreement, we find ourselves pushing or shutting people down, unsure of how to find any kind of resolution with them.

When our ego is in the attached state, we experience:

- Defensiveness without willingness to compromise
- Blame and criticism of others without taking responsibility for ourselves
- Lack of willingness to consider another perspective
- Projection of our feelings and experiences onto others

Think about where you've experienced this on social media, either within yourself or from others. Have you ever DM'd with someone who was unwilling to have a healthy debate or conflict with you and just wanted to express how much they thought you were wrong? Have you ever judged another Content Creator for being a part of the problem, criticizing how they use their platform without considering their point of view? Remember that we've all got egos and that the ego will usually come out when someone feels threatened, angry, scared, insecure, or overwhelmed. The ego operates on the level of self-protection and separateness rather than vulnerability and togetherness.

When you feel that strong pull to defend yourself, blame someone or something else, or double down hard on your position without compromise, it could be a sign that you're feeling threatened in your sense of identity and safety in the world. For example, being misunderstood or lied about online can be a very disorienting experience, especially if being misunderstood or invalidated is at the root of your trauma. A huge part of the learning process here is to find a way to acknowledge that your own need to be understood and validated is a form of self-protection but does not need to run the show into your adulthood.

The term "ego death" refers to the process of dropping the whole dance between puffing yourself up and making yourself small. It's the moment when you can see beyond good–bad, right–wrong binaries and stop trying to be right, opting instead to try to feel at peace. A part of that process can feel like a small "death" because we're internally releasing an identity that once protected us and kept us safe but is no longer supportive in our growth. Letting yourself be misunderstood by people might feel like letting go of years and years of stress from constantly making sure people understood you.

Although the ego's intentions are to protect, we have to recognize it for what it is—a part of our mind that doesn't *need* to run our entire lives. Our consciousness is stronger than those instincts the ego has to hide, shrink, or puff up. When you can see that there's more to us beyond the ego's game, you'll start to view yourself as a far more whole and expanded person. The ego isn't going anywhere, so let's learn to work with it.

There are three core ego patterns we can observe within ourselves. Let's begin by seeing if you can identify any of these patterns within yourself.

Ego Pattern 1: Forming Identities and Roles to Solidify Our Place in the World

The internal freak-out I had from identifying as an author is an example of one of the ways the ego attempts to maintain familiarity and sameness—by clinging tightly to the identities we've subconsciously taken on as who we are and who we aren't. In that moment, the immediate thoughts that popped up in my head were *But I'm just an Instagram influencer, not an author. I'm just an online coach, not an author.* Notice how these thoughts are self-deflating thoughts—making "influencer" and "coach" inferior to "author." By buying into the belief that I was "only an influencer and coach, not an author," I would have been able to stay extremely comfortable doing the same thing I'd been doing for years. Taking on the identity of "author" wasn't just a simple moment of deciding I was going to write a book. Becoming an author included facing all the parts of myself that didn't believe I was good enough to be one—including doubts around my abilities as a writer and, most of all, the fear of being found out as a total fraud. None of these was an easy internal fear to navigate. But in order to grow and do things we've never done, we each need to find our own ways of integrating a new identity—just like I did when I decided that I was, in fact, an author.

> "Every action you take is a vote for the type of person you wish to become. No single instance will transform your beliefs, but as the votes build up, so does the evidence of your new identity."
>
> JAMES CLEAR, *ATOMIC HABITS*

Identities are what help us feel protected in the world—because identities tell us how to act and where we belong. Stanford University professor and neuroscientist Dr. Andrew Huberman mentioned in a recent podcast episode[2] that there are identity-based habits we can develop that help us build the larger picture of ourselves. Posting on social media in a particular way is one of the largest identity-based habits a Creator can adopt. What you post, how often you post, and how you use and experience social media places you in a certain subset (or niche) of the internet almost immediately and automatically. You become *someone* in an industry, and that means *something.*

Identity Exercise

Grab your journal, open to a fresh page, and answer the questions below.

What are some of the identities that have helped you maintain the status quo?

Think about the identities you've had throughout your life—specifically the ones that have helped you stay safe, comfortable, and in familiar territory.

Some of mine include:

- The super nice, nonjudgmental person
- The person who "never gets angry"
- The smart girl who went to nursing school
- The noncreative person

What are some of the identities you've needed to adopt over the years to help you grow?

Now think about the identities you've taken on that were uncomfortable but helped you learn more about yourself, your skills, and your potential and helped you become more fully seen.

Some of mine include:

- The fitness competitor
- The social media influencer
- The YouTube vlogger

- The entrepreneur
- The author

How did your ego kick and scream before you fully embodied and adopted these identites?

Which parts of yourself did you have to face to adopt these identities?

Which beliefs and habits did you finally let go of so that you could step into these new roles?

For me, the small-town, noncreative, super-agreeable people pleaser within me had to die. Without that, I couldn't step into the growth-inducing, edge-pushing, polarizing influencer and, eventually, the author I've become.

Ask yourself: What habits do you need to form next in order to more fully claim the identity of the person you want to be? What beliefs have you needed to adopt? What decisions will you now start to make? What actions will you take? What creations and ideas will you bring to life with your new identity?

Journal your answer to each of these questions. Really sit with each of the answers, noticing how much you've grown already—and recognizing how possible it is to grow even more in the future. Consider: What identities do you want to adopt for yourself in this next season of your journey as a Content Creator?

Being a Content Creator constantly challenges us to adopt new identities that help us grow. It forces us to question whether or not we're "the kind of person who . . ."

- is in the public eye
- posts pictures of themselves

- others are influenced by
- talks about edgy topics on the internet in front of strangers

Social media's presence in our lives helps us become aware of what we *could* grow into, if we chose to do so. There's a lot of opportunities not only to grow into a bigger, more influential, and well-known Creator but also to try on different identities you see other people embodying for yourself, maybe in areas you never knew existed! Take, for example, the person who never saw themself as a Content Creator but who, once TikTok was released, finally found a format where they could create their hilarious political skits. Those skits went viral on their account, providing them an audience of hundreds of thousands within a few months of starting. Or consider the person who started a podcast about their holistic-healing journey with chronic illness to express the impact it's had on them, eventually and accidentally becoming a voice and inspiration for countless others. Take a moment to ask yourself what identities you've recognized within yourself since being on social media that have helped you grow. Have you claimed the sexy/sensual identity? The intelligent-teacher identity? The free-spirited identity?

As much as social media helps us find new identities to grow into, it also anchors and reaffirms our current identities. Often, people with similar lifestyles, jobs, traumas, hobbies, or stories migrate to one another and validate each other's experiences—like a group of peers going through something similar. This is why being *followed* often feels so good. A community of people who like what you like and care about what you care about? What an incredible thing. The flip side of being validated regularly in your experience is that it can often feel difficult to transcend or grow out of that experience because you've attracted a group of people who followed you for that thing you once identified with. If it was a challenge to evolve as a person before, social media adds this layer to that identity-evolution process of knowing that there's a whole group of people you'll share it with who may not follow along.

Ego Pattern 2: Defending Our Limiting Behavior Patterns

I remember reading the book *Quiet: The Power of Introverts in a World That Can't Stop Talking* by Susan Cain in 2018. As a self-identified introvert, I took *so* much comfort in reading that book. Every word validated my choices to stay in rather than go out, be a "grandma," and even ghost people when I didn't want to deal with the potential discomfort and conflict that could arise from directly declining invitations. I clung to the idea that extroverts were "not my kind of person." It wasn't until I spent an entire week at Burning Man that I began to reevaluate my identity as an introvert. Burning Man is a week-long art-and-music festival experience in the deserts of Nevada. With eighty thousand people, it's one of the most highly social and stimulating events in the world. And there I was, spending all day and night with so many people—and new people, at that! For the first time in my life, I didn't leave an event like that feeling drained; rather, I was energized, revitalized, and more inspired than ever before.

I began to wake up to the way my ego was clinging to my identity of being an introvert. Being an introvert armed me with the perfect excuse to not interact with or meet new people, lean into connection, or put myself in uncomfortable social situations. Over the following three years, I found myself in a relationship with an extremely social partner who valued squeezing the most juice out of life, pulling all-nighters, and maximizing experiences with people as much as possible. And then there was me—hitting my supposed social "max" by one AM.

As much as I vehemently protested, defending my choices to stay home or leave early, there was a part of me that began intently questioning why I *so badly* wanted my introvert identity to be true. I asked myself, "Is there an experience I'm missing out on as a result of constantly defending this identity? Are there creative options available to me that I don't want to see? What am I gaining from clinging to my introvert identity? Is it actually worth it?"

This line of questioning and introspection led me to realize that when I'm on a cozy couch around people with whom I can deeply connect and have intimate conversations, I can absolutely enjoy the *hell* out of myself far past one AM. I also realized that getting lost in the thought spiral of how horrible I'd feel the next day if I didn't "optimize my sleep" actually drained my energy far more than an enjoyable social situation ever could. Now I value late-night talks and dance experiences with friends—while still being attuned to my boundaries and not losing my ability to say no if I *truly* want to.

The ego fiercely defends its sense of comfort and control in the familiarity of what we've come to know. This is one of the strongest forces that hold people back from changing their behavior patterns. Sometimes, this may mean defending your beliefs and ideas that actually limit you. You might hate your voice so much that you could *never* host a podcast, or you might prioritize giving your audience so much of your time and energy completely for free while finding yourself constantly drained, or maybe you pride yourself on being self-made and never ask for help when it comes to growing your audience. In my story, my ego clung to the idea that I was an introvert so that it didn't have to confront the real truth: *I didn't know how to be myself around people I didn't feel comfortable with.* This isn't true for everyone who identifies as an introvert, but it was for me. Ask yourself: How many beliefs do you cling to like this one, especially when it comes to your potential as a Content Creator? Isn't it so alluring and seductive to buy into a particular identity so that we never have to step outside of our comfort zone?

When you realize that your ego is defending its usual patterns of behavior, you're more easily able to take a step back and ask yourself these types of questions:

- Is it possible that I'm wrong about this identity?
- What am I so scared will happen if I stop defending this pattern?
- Is there another option that could make my life even better?
- What creative solutions can I come up with to keep what I care about the same while expanding my capacity?

Ego Pattern 3: Deflecting Personal Responsibility

The other way the ego maintains the status quo is by hijacking your analysis of emotions and thoughts. Remember: it either *inflates* itself or *deflates* itself as an attempt to deflect taking personal responsibility.

Personal responsibility is the notion that, as adults, we are individually responsible for our behaviors, responses, choices, decisions, actions, and energy. Other people, the external world, and situations can trigger feelings within us, but they are not responsible for managing those emotions. We are ultimately the full stewards of our own experience.

Deflecting Personal Responsibility	Taking Personal Responsibility
Inflated Ego: "I am so much better than that person in that topic—I should have more followers." **Deflated Ego:** "That person is so much better than me at that—who am I to even try?"	"That person may have more followers than me and may be doing an amazing job—but I can acknowledge that observing them is bringing up some insecurity in me about my own abilities to create that kind of success. Although those fears are present, I know—deep down—that I'm capable of doing the same. My fears and insecurities may be present, but I know it's truly up to me to create what I want."

In the inflated-ego state, you may notice yourself (or others) declaring superiority or "rightness." The "I'm right, you're wrong—you're small, I'm big" argument is the ego's attempt to make itself bigger and not take personal responsibility for its own greatness. In the above example, the ego doesn't want to acknowledge its insecurities about not having as many followers as someone else, and perhaps this is a convenient way for an individual to avoid doing the additional work to learn how to grow their own audience.

In the deflated-ego state, you may notice yourself (or others) declaring inferiority. The "They're better than me, who am I to even try?" argument is the deflated ego's attempt to do the exact same thing the inflated ego does: avoid taking personal responsibility for its own greatness. If it took responsibility, it'd then have to acknowledge its insecurities, self-doubt, and worthiness patterns. It'd need to shift out of the ego and into the authentic self to do this. You'd be that active operator of said shift—using your awareness and intention to change the direction of your mind and guiding yourself into that process of facing your insecurities and doing the scary thing.

Whether we're *defending* our identity and behavior patterns or *deflecting* personal responsibility, the ego automatically reacts to its greatest fear: *losing itself.* Having its identity shattered. Losing the illusion of control it clings to. Admitting to being wrong. And ultimately: *seeing itself.* Taking responsibility for ourselves can feel difficult, especially if it means:

- Not justifying, blaming, deflecting, or defending
- Asking for help
- Acknowledging insecurities
- Doing those things we've been avoiding
- Facing our fears

If you're a Content Creator, you'll be facing this subtle inner-world conflict most days. Will you succumb to your ego's attempts to keep you small, or will you break past them and choose a more empowering story and sequence of actions? Social media is a place that can help us grow a healthy ego, but the line between that and becoming deeply attached to our ego is fine as hell. How easy is it to feel justified to a bunch of strangers who are judging you based on the content *you* choose to share about you—when you know it doesn't share the whole picture? How often do you find yourself justifying not posting, not going live, or not sharing the content that matters to you because of how you may be perceived?

Here's what I've learned: being able to separate from your ego, look at it for what it is, and take personal responsibility for your experience is going to be the biggest game changer for you. Without it, you render yourself powerless to endless comparison, fear of being judged (and actually being judged), and getting canceled. You'll find it difficult to not succumb to the pressure to "keep up," the resistance to make pivots, the fear of speaking your truth, and the ability to do what you're actually on social media to do: express yourself, help people, and reclaim your self-sovereignty by carving out your own personalized corner of the internet that'll change your entire life.

TAKING THE DRIVER'S SEAT AND MAKING YOUR EGO YOUR ALLY

Now that you know what you're working with when it comes to your own ego, you can really start wielding this new information as a tool to help you grow and become more in control over your inner experience. The ego is automatic—just like how your body breathes automatically—but, similar to breathing, you can consciously work with it to improve your experience. Let's practice taking the mental driver's seat and make your ego your ally using this exercise below.

Becoming the Witness Exercise

Start by observing your breathing without making any changes or adjustments. See how your body simply breathes—keeping you alive, entirely automatically. Then, take a few deep breaths. See what it feels like to breathe in through your nose and out through your mouth—and then to breathe into your belly, filling it, and then releasing out through your mouth.

Begin to observe your thoughts by closing your eyes for one to two minutes, and just watch. See as those thoughts go by like clouds. Some thoughts may invoke an emotion—frustration, annoyance, sadness, guilt, joy, or delight. The stronger the emotions and memories associated with those thoughts, the more attachment you may feel to the stories your mind tells you about them. Say to yourself: "That is a thought, but I am not that thought—the thought simply exists and is passing by right now. It doesn't mean anything about who I am. I don't have to believe it as truth."

Did you notice any changes when you said that to yourself? Any shifts in emotions or in your body? Perhaps you relaxed just a smidge more than you had before. That's you separating yourself from your ego, regaining control over your internal experience.

To deepen this practice and work with your ego, review these mantras below and add them to your toolbox.

- I am *not* this thought—I am experiencing this thought.
- I am *not* my body—I have a body.
- I am *not* my achievements—I have earned these achievements.
- I am *not* my feelings—I am experiencing my feelings.
- I am *not* my career—I have developed skills in a particular structure and construct.
- I am *not* my relationship with other people—I experience myself and the world through my relationships with other people.
- I am *not* my history and trauma—I have memories and pain from the past, which do not define me in the present or future.

When you pause and pay attention to what's happening in your mind and body using your breath and awareness, you create space and become able to view things just a little more clearly. There is power in your pause because it reminds you that you are the experiencer, sitting in the driver's seat. *That* version of yourself is the one with all the leverage—because it provides you the awareness of your own autonomy and sovereignty in making your own choices and creating your own reality from the inside out. At the core, transformation and growth comes down to asking these questions in the space between your awareness and your action:

- Can I observe my pattern and choose differently?
- Can I see that I can still be a good person while doing the controversial, "edgy" thing that might not fit within the parameters of acceptability I previously believed were necessary?

Think about it like this: it's not about "killing" our ego or getting rid of our ego in any way—it's more about having a slow, tolerable process of bringing awareness to the ego when we're faced with a growth opportunity. It's about sitting at the edge of what feels safe, acceptable, normal, or comfortable and slowly but surely pushing those edges out. And once you're there, then you're in a place to feel less restricted in what kinds of behavior, thoughts, roles, and identities can be "you."

THE TOOLS IN YOUR TOOLBOX

When I sit and think about you—the reader, the Content Creator—I feel a deep sense of camaraderie. I don't know how you grew up, your life experiences, or what kind of content you create. But I know the types of experiences you're going through as a Content Creator—or what you will go through in your journey—*deep in my bones*. Many of you will build massive communities of like-minded people who will read and become influenced by everything you do and say. Some of you will get canceled or publicly called out, which will lead you to finding your way to reestablishing trust with your audience. Others of you will monetize your platforms, add streams of revenue, and find a sense of purpose. The outcomes and possibilities are endless—but so are the challenges you'll face. Regardless of what social media throws at you, having command over your inner world with different mindsets and emotional tools in your toolbox is one of the best things you can do to support yourself while riding the waves.

four

Keeping Up with the Influencers

It was 2015, and I'd just decided to go full-time as a fitness influencer and online coach. My entire day revolved around sharing myself with my audience through the content I created. That audience was growing so fast—daily, *by the hundreds*—that brand deals and client inquiries often flooded my inbox faster than I could keep up with.

I was in my early twenties—and having just moved across the country to Los Angeles, I didn't have many relationships or responsibilities outside of my burgeoning online presence. I was fairly shy and didn't go out much, so all of my friends were other influencers who I'd met online. We bonded over our shared life path, the successes and challenges we'd faced along the way. My audience became my community—the people with whom I bonded, socialized, and found belonging.

For a while, this experience was purely incredible. It felt *magical* to watch new people follow my page every day. I received hundreds of messages each week from my followers detailing how my videos were inspiring them in their own journeys. I found it so *cool* that being a person people knew, listened to, and enjoyed following was something that was possible for me—never mind so beneficial for other people. Ah, wow. What a time it was to be an influencer.

The internet was by no means young, but that specific corner of it—in which YouTube Creators developed personal brands related to specific niches (like fitness)—was developing in real time. Social media platforms often have a life cycle, which usually includes a few specific boom periods during which explosive growth is possible. My career happened to begin at a period of transition, when Instagram was overtaking Facebook as the default platform and the culture of YouTube infotainment was picking up. I quickly set about learning everything I could to be successful, and because we were in the right place at the right time, my influencer contemporaries and I got to play a part in pioneering the path of what it looked like to build an Instagram and YouTube following. It was all uncharted territory. Everyone in that early Creator cohort was taking it one step at a time without knowing what lay ahead. None of us was given any disclaimers, warnings, or tools to navigate the journey of being *followed*.

As an influencer, my brand's success was predicated on how appealing my content was—not just in the value of the fitness information I shared but also in the intimacy inherent in the way I shared it. Each video was a window into my life, an opportunity for the audience to both connect with Amanda the person and become more invested in Amanda Bucci, the brand. The series I became most known for was called *That Prep Life* (2016), following the journey of my bikini-competition prep—training, nutrition, thoughts, feelings, challenges, experiences, and travel. The series closely matched the basic structure of Joseph Campbell's model of the monomyth, or Hero's Journey, a storytelling framework that also mirrors stages of human experience. The hero (me) had to answer the call to adventure, meet with their mentor, go through tests, train and prepare, and ultimately culminate the journey with a battle or moment of truth.

For me, the journey was a twenty-week fitness-competition prep that included a nutrition plan and fitness program. I hired a coach, got into a training program, and religiously tracked nutritional intake. Each Sunday, I prepped my meals and filled my refrigerator with the food I needed. Five months of training culminated in what Campbell would call the Ordeal: a series of three bikini competitions. As I went along, I shared every step with my audience. I recorded and posted all my workouts, struggling with the side effects of hard-core dieting. Posting four or five videos each week, I brought my viewers on the journey with me, giving them access to the highs and the lows. Looking back, it was a bit like a TV show—season finale and all—which is why it felt so hard to be the one to have to cancel it.

Imagine the way you usually watch a reality TV show, judging the cast members and thinking, "If it were me, I would *definitely* do things differently." Now, imagine you're the star of the show *and* the producer. All of your audience members can comment whatever opinions they have—anonymously. I wasn't fully aware of it at the time, but sharing such an intimate experience of my life and myself, where people were able to make unfiltered commentary, extraordinarily impacted how I felt about myself and the decisions I made.

As much as I enjoyed the praise, opportunity, and community I built, it felt difficult to post about anything outside of my predefined brand without feeling like my every move was being judged. Deep down, I just wanted to eat and work out without having so much structure and focus on how I went about doing that. I didn't want to stay stuck performing the behaviors of what was "on brand" for "fitness influencer Amanda." I craved to stop setting fitness goals altogether, heal my relationship with food, and do so without putting that whole process on display for the whole world. But my fitness journey (and how my body looked) were so inextricably linked to my income, brand partnerships, and business that it often felt impossible to break free from that box.

I knew there was untapped potential inside of me—dying to come out and offer more than what I'd been giving. There was a sea of words, experiences, businesses, offerings, creations, and messages within me, bursting at the seams but held back by a buckling dam of expectations and pressure to maintain my brand as a fitness influencer. But a moving river cannot stay behind a dam for too long without cracks appearing or the dam breaking altogether—just like how your honest, raw, authentic truth of where you want to go and what you want to do can't stay repressed forever without finding a way out.

Eventually, I found the courage within myself to slowly stop recording my workouts, taking a picture every time I trained, and sharing my fitness goals. What I once freely offered up to the public, I slowly pulled back on, and I reclaimed more of my privacy. I'd previously shared almost everything about my process—including my experience with anxiety, the stresses of my competition and intense training, and the challenges I had dealing with rude and judgmental comments online. But because these new changes felt bigger, deeper, and more personal, it felt important to put up some additional barriers around myself before I so willingly shared those parts with people so quickly. Instead of fitness, I found interest in business and social media growth. I started posting infographics instead of body photos and watched my likes drop from twenty thousand to five thousand per post. People joked that I was "losing my mojo" and becoming less popular and interesting because my likes had dropped. But feeling free to create and write what felt authentic to me felt so good, it didn't even matter to me to hear people say that—because I knew it wasn't true. I hadn't lost my mojo; I was just getting started.

WHY WE FEEL THE PRESSURE TO KEEP UP

In a 2021 *Vox* article, writer Emily Stewart interviewed Boston College sociologist Juliet Schor about the root of American consumerism. Schor claimed,

> The key impetus for contemporary consumer society has been the growth of inequality, the existence of unequal social structures, and the role that consumption came to play in establishing people's position in

that unequal hierarchy. For many people, it's about consuming to their social position, and trying to keep up with their social position.[3]

This phenomenon is what we know as "keeping up with the Joneses," or trying to consume as much as the people to whom we compare ourselves in an effort to maintain a perception and identity of value and social currency. By the 1920s, there was a boom of mass production in the industrial world, leading to mass consumption in society, and being seen by your neighbor to have a particular car, house, or clothes suddenly became very important. It was a status symbol to show you had, in fact, *made it.* The simple idea that you were being *seen* by others in a favorable light was the motivational impetus to achieve and buy those status symbols. When it comes to social media, that same social programming has become infused into how we approach content creation, brand management, and, of course, brand perception.

This is what I call "keeping up with the influencers."

> "We buy things we don't need with money we don't have to impress people we don't like."
>
> CHUCK PALAHNIUK, *FIGHT CLUB*

The internet itself provided rocket fuel to consumerism and the drive to keep up with the people we compare ourselves to. All of a sudden, we were able to be in contact with a much larger group of people on a constant, infinite loop of never-ending feeds. Schor calls these people we're in contact with and compare ourselves to "reference groups"—formerly represented by neighbors and coworkers but now extending to millions of other Content Creators around the globe.

Whether it's Fitness Chad, Business Brenda, or Molly the Supermom, every industry experiences its own version of this by being aware of who the "top" Creators in its space are, what they're doing, and how they stack up in comparison. It's no longer just houses, cars, and careers—it's how white your house is, how well designed your graphics are, how many other popular people in your industry you collaborate with, and even how socially conscious you are. I'm in both the online-coaching business and personal-development spaces, and I've noticed how the types of expectations people have of others are evolving and becoming more nuanced. People are even concerned with how much therapy a Creator has had, or how much they seem to genuinely care about their audience. Some of the most successful Creators seem to be living extremely balanced lives while also making a lot of money, doing lots of inner work, having plenty of fun, and creating content all the time. In my niche, "keeping up with the influencers" is not just about having all of the material items but also about embodying the balanced, successful, healed person. If you feel as though what you're doing is never enough—you're not alone.

Take a moment to grab your journal and reflect on where you may be feeling outside pressure from social media by answering the below questions:

- Who in your industry do you feel pressure to keep up with?
- What kind of ideals do you feel expected to keep up with in order to gain the kind of success others have or be perceived by your audience to be in the top-tier groups?
- How does that perception affect the way you create content, the things you do to please your audience, or the parts of yourself you keep hidden to not look like an outcast?

The pressure can be unrelenting when you make any kind of change with a following watching you—but two of my most pivotal moments in my journey were when I released the pressure and expectations I felt before making pivots that felt very authentic to my journey. First, I let go of being one of the top fitness YouTubers at the time, and then, years later, I let go of my "seven-figure entrepreneur" material-success status. Letting go of these two statuses required me to let go of the narrative I held that said, "In order to be more respected and credible, you not only have to achieve at high standards but also must maintain those achievements—or else you'll be viewed as a failure." If you've ever felt like you've needed to maintain a certain image to make sure others perceive you in a positive light, you've probably needed to face a lot of emotion and fear around that, too. Have you ever avoided taking a social media break to stay relevant or hidden a mistake you made from your audience to prevent them from potentially seeing you as less than a credible authority? Maybe you're still maintaining that image, or maybe you've already let people see you break or be in the middle of your process.

The starting point for most of us is caring what other people think of us. That's okay—and completely normal. On a deep level, humans crave the approval of our parents, our mentors, our peers, and our audiences because it reminds us that we belong and that we're accepted. But no matter what you achieve on the path to keeping up with those expectations and impossible standards, one lesson you'll inevitably learn is that—no matter what you do—you cannot please everybody. Although it's an emotional challenge to deal with people not liking you or accepting you in whatever ways you feel are best on social media, it's one of the most worthwhile paths to recognize that just existing—exactly as you are—is going to create contrast for someone out there. Maybe you used to be an alcoholic and AA saved you, but you ended up finding that some of the AA twelve-step process doesn't fully align with you, leading you to seek other modalities of healing, and now you can drink or use other substances in moderation. Perhaps you built an entire YouTube channel on being a vegan, only to later realize that veganism doesn't align with your body's physiological needs and health—so you decided to integrate meat back into your diet for health purposes. In both of these situations, the Creator embarks on a path of authentic growth and thriving, but some of their audience members may feel upset, judgmental, or critical of that pathway if it directly conflicts with their own beliefs. Humans are complex beings—and this kind of nuance and complexity is coming out from Creators more and more the longer we're online and growing as people.

You will have just as many haters and critics (which we'll discuss in chapter eight) doing what feels authentic and makes you happy as you would if you were doing the thing that pleases others. On the authentic path, you will also have just as many people—the right people, *your* people!—appreciating you, truly seeing you, and meeting you where you're at with gratitude and love. Of course, this is an important North Star in theory—but deprogramming your mind and actions from societal conditioning takes work. Let's dive into guiding principles and action steps to support your shift from being primarily led by the expectations of others to leading yourself based on your own values.

GETTING OUT FROM UNDER THE INFLUENCE

According to former Harvard psychologist Dr. Robert Kegan's theory of adult development, becoming an "adult" is the process of transitioning to higher stages of development. It involves developing an independent sense of self and increasing in wisdom and social maturity. This looks like becoming more self-aware and in control of our behavior, as well as being better able to manage our relationships and other social factors.[4] Kegan claims that transformation isn't about learning new ideas but about changing our perspective of the world. My spiritual-psychology professors, Ron and Mary Hulnick, said it best when they coined the phrase: "How you relate to the issue *is* the issue."

In contemplating the question "How do I let go of what others think of me?" we have to look at the different forces that have affected our relationship to a comparison with others. How you grew up, your culture, family and social dynamics, social power structures, privilege, inequality, inequity, misogyny, white supremacy, and bigotry, for starters, can affect how deeply you've learned or needed to care about other people's opinions. Let's talk about the process for minimizing how much you care about what other people think about you and how much it affects your actions so that you can grow as a Content Creator and feel more free to be yourself over time.

Embrace the Part That Cares

Rather than trying to push away the part of you that cares about what other people think, start by embracing the fact that—right now—you *do* care about what other people think, and that's okay. It's not bad or wrong to care about what others think—it's more about acknowledging how those beliefs are currently affecting your freedom to live life on your own terms. Try saying this: "I accept that I care about what other people think, and that's okay." How did saying that feel? If you felt even a tiny bit more relaxed than you did before, it's because you just started integrating a part of yourself that you've previously rejected, helping you feel a little more whole.

Practice Releasing Judgment Against Yourself, Others, and Situations

In my spiritual-psychology program at the University of Santa Monica, we learned various strategies for emotional transformation—but one strategy we repeated over and over and that was infused into every lesson: *letting go of judgment*. Judgment can act as this filmy top layer, sitting just above our real emotions, preventing us from truly accessing the more honest and authentic feelings we have. For example: if we're judging someone who has a bigger following than us as coming across as *fake* and *inauthentic*, the judgment is really acting as a protective barrier between us and the true underlying feeling. The emotion underneath the judgment could be something a little more difficult to face, like low self-esteem or not feeling good enough in comparison to that person. Remember: most judgments of others are really judgments of yourself—and judgments against yourself generally perpetuate mental and emotional anguish. The good news is that judgments can be cleared when we recognize that we're all doing the best with the tools we have. To release judgment requires us to move out of the ego and into our hearts.

Let's say someone wrote a really shitty comment below one of your videos. Maybe your brain automatically tells you, "This person's trash" or "They're just jealous and insecure." If you're in the *energy of judgment* against that person, it doesn't provide any room to learn and grow from that moment—nor does it lead you toward peace. It may temporarily protect you from pain, but it doesn't get to the root of that pain. A simple prompt to practice is filling in the second half of this sentence: "I forgive myself for judging myself, others, or this situation as . . . (insert judgments here), and the truth is . . . (everyone is doing their best, it's okay for me to be a human, this person is probably also in pain, etc.)." This is called *compassionate self-forgiveness*—a practice originating from the spiritual-psychology program at the University of Santa Monica. It seems simple, but actually taking a few minutes to do this in your own life will remind you that we are all still learning, growing, making mistakes, being human, doing our best, and having our own experiences.

> "Not giving a fuck does not mean being indifferent; it means being comfortable with being different."
>
> MARK MANSON, *THE SUBTLE ART OF NOT GIVING A FUCK*

Release Attachment to Controlling Your Metrics

After years of watching my audience size grow, the first time I began losing followers was a shock. When I shifted my content, it felt like, all of a sudden,

I had done something entirely wrong. Although I knew my change in content would filter out the people who weren't aligned with my new direction, I still had to grapple with feeling like every post I made where I lost followers represented a mistake or doing something wrong. For a moment, I found myself hyperaware of the number of likes, comments, and shares any post got—feeling pangs of self-doubt when a thoughtful graphic only received a fifth of the likes that a picture of my body received. I quickly realized I had no real control over how people reacted to me. As much as there are ways to will more followers to your page—like posting multiple times a day or joining some questionable (likely paid) giveaway group—if you're committed to being authentic in your posts and creation, it's a timely opportunity to find more comfort in releasing attachment to controlling those metrics.

Whether it's Buddhism, stoicism, or simply "not giving a fuck," practicing nonattachment is a principle that can help you release stress and anxiety around the uncontrollable factors of social media. Notice if you feel anxiety or stress building up in your body when you think about those numbers. What is your brain making that mean about you? What fears are present? If that feeling inside of you could speak, what would it say? Are those thoughts 100 percent true, 100 percent of the time? Simultaneously, guide yourself into looking at those numbers and say, "That doesn't matter as much as I think it does. How can I be more accepting of these fluctuations right now?"

Increase Your Tolerance for Uncertainty

Certainty is a core human need each of us has to feel generally safe in the world—but we can seldom be certain when it comes to how people will react to us or if an outcome we want will absolutely happen! Adopting a healthy relationship with uncertainty helps us to minimize stress when situations feel out of our control. To practice increasing your tolerance for uncertainty, start by taking a low-stakes action that feels like the right combination of authentic and a little scary. Below is a process for taking those small yet impactful steps to social media growth even in the face of uncertainty:

- Step 1: Decide what action you'll take, like saying something controversial, sharing a piece of your story, or going live for the first time.
- Step 2: Take note of how you feel before taking action and acknowledge any resistance you may have to taking that step.
- Step 3: Take a few breaths and remind yourself that you are inherently resourceful and capable of navigating what may happen.
- Step 4: Then, do the thing. Allow yourself space to process anything that comes up after you post.
- Step 5: Repeat this process as often as feels tolerable.

Define Your Intention and Release the "When" and the "How"

Being clear on your desires is a major part of actually receiving what you want—so if you want a bigger audience, more notoriety in your space, or to get on a certain podcast, clarify what that would look and feel like to you. Being an active participant in creating what you want starts with wholeheartedly believing with every cell in your body that what you desire is on its way to you and then releasing attachment to how quickly or in what way it might arrive. Releasing the "when" and the "how" is helpful, as these are two factors that seem as though they're in our control but are actually unknowns. We can control our actions and how we show up to the game but not the outcomes or the speed at which they come. Believing that we can control getting what we want within a certain timeline is rooted in the ego's need for certainty and security.

When you set your intentions and clarify what you want, the next steps are to take *aligned and intentional action* in the direction of that desire. Intentionality, trust, and alignment provide the context for how you move through the action-taking process. Every action step you take toward your goal gets to be an opportunity to learn—about marketing, copywriting, video editing, and, most importantly, yourself. Learning, developing skills, and staying in motion are what help you reach those goals you've got.

The above lays out a very simplified version of the process of *manifesting*—which is a concept rooted in being an active participant in creating what you want rather than waiting for it to come to you. Manifesting can't be discussed without acknowledging that every person has different levels of accessibility, trauma, and privilege. So much of the "keeping up with the influencers (Joneses)" phenomenon is rooted in white supremacy and privilege. The idea that anyone can create a social media platform and become successful is technically true, but those who have the most ease and speed in gaining success typically have the most privilege.

For example, as an attractive white woman in a heteronormative-presenting relationship (although I've come out to my audience as polyamorous and bisexual), it's important to acknowledge that the privileges I possess have benefited me in growing an audience and achieving success. Acknowledging my own privilege has become an important piece to share because it helps any audience member of mine contextualize my story, especially when it comes to learning from me or following in my footsteps to success. In considering your own process for creating what you desire, remember to question and review the privilege and lived experience of any Content Creator you may compare yourself to.

Enjoy the Process, Not Just the Outcome

When you focus your attention on what you're learning and experiencing every step of the way, your day-to-day life becomes more fulfilling and joyful. Allow social media to be a place you actually get value from, every single day—rather than another boring item on your to-do list that you have to check off in order to make progress or be "successful." We'll discuss more about how to do this in the next chapter!

REGULATE YOUR EMOTIONS

Learning how to become an active participant in bringing yourself to states of more calm and regulation during moments of overwhelm, stress, anxiety, fear, anger, or other emotions is a skill that's not only beneficial as a Content Creator but also as a person. Regulating your emotions is the process of adjusting, balancing, and modulating our inner world through tools like breathwork, meditation, shaking, movement, co-regulation in healthy relationships, mindfulness, and more. Think of this practice as training for your nervous system—the system of your body that regulates your emotional state. If, for example, sharing about your cannabis use feels like an important next step but simultaneously makes you want to *vomit*, any step in that direction is going to stretch you. Your body might start to contract, you might make up narratives as to why you shouldn't, or you might even project your anger onto other Creators who openly share about their own cannabis use. The more you learn to breathe through the discomfort and regulate the sensations in your body, the more resilience you'll build within your nervous system to tolerate being on the edge of your comfort zone—including any social media shares that feel nerve wracking. It's important to note that some of these edgier shares may activate a trauma trigger, so if something is feeling intense or overwhelming, seek professional support before taking action.

The below is a simple process you can use whenever you feel emotions arise in your body from being on social media.

1. Bring awareness to your feeling, and then define, locate, or identify what you're experiencing. If you aren't sure how to name a particular emotion, it's helpful to start by naming sensations in the body, such as tightness in the chest, fogginess in the mind, shakiness in your limbs, warmth in the face, and so on. This allows you to practice awareness of what's going on in your body and leads you to understand what emotions may be present.

Another tool to use is to personify that sensation as a part of you or as a sub-personality (like Irene the Inner Critic or Jordan the Judgy Teenager). We are made up of an infinite number of parts that each play a different role in our lives. Giving them a name, title, color, texture, or more tangible form allows you to see those parts of you as distinct and separate and will help you interact with them more easily.

Remember to get curious and try to stay open, compassionate, and nonjudgmental.

2. Investigate what lives in that space. An easy question to ask yourself is "What is this sensation trying to tell me?" or "What does this part of me need?" Give yourself time, space, compassion, and grace when asking these questions. Use a journal to write, or just sit in silence with yourself if that feels like a safe option. You can also practice this process with a trusted facilitator or professional or some other nonjudgmental person in your life.
3. Express and acknowledge the emotions that exist and the parts of you that are present in the moment. Pretending that feelings aren't there doesn't make them go away; it just hides them away until they come out later. Be as honest with yourself about what you're feeling as you can be.
4. Integrate. Healing is being able to increase emotional safety in areas that previously felt unsafe, triggering, or scary. Think of the simple statement "Taking a breath is a radical act against your pattern." The action steps you can take after you uncover a pattern are essentially whatever actions you'd rather be taking (or experiences you'd rather be having) in small, tolerable steps. Perhaps you want to worry less about what other people think of you when you post. The person who is less bothered by social media comments posts what they want in a way that feels good to them. In the moments you'd rather hide, share. Start in low-stakes, tolerable ways if certain

> actions feel too overwhelming for you. Perhaps you can create a private account or only share specific experiences or ideas with close friends first. And don't forget: you don't need to do anything that feels too overwhelming.

Head to followedbook.io to grab a ten-minute meditation to use whenever you want to detach from external pressures and reconnect to yourself.

EMBODYING YOUR VALUES

In his best-selling book *The 7 Habits of Highly Effective People,* Stephen Covey introduced the "Be, Do, Have" model as a framework that highly effective people use to achieve goals. Rather than asking, "What do I need to have in order to do what I want to do and in order to feel how I want to feel?" it asks, "Who do I need to be in order to do what I want to do, which will help me have what I want to have?"

I implement this specific framework with my business and life-coaching clients by having them define their core drivers and values. Many people deeply value their space, their privacy, and their freedom to do what they desire, without adding layers of pressure and expectation on top of that. Some are heavily driven by legacy, wealth, and leaving the world a better place than it was when they came here—for their families or otherwise. Some are motivated by fun, pleasure, and play. Others deeply value experiences, connections, and relationships. When you actually define what you value and how you want to be, it will lead you directly toward what actions to take that align with those values.

Beginning with *being* rather than *doing* or *having* flips our current societal standards on their head. The "keeping up with the influencers" phenomenon is one small example of how societal conditioning teaches us that we need to have things—money, success, fame, credibility, marriage—before we can feel the way we want to feel (happy, fulfilled, loving, open-hearted).

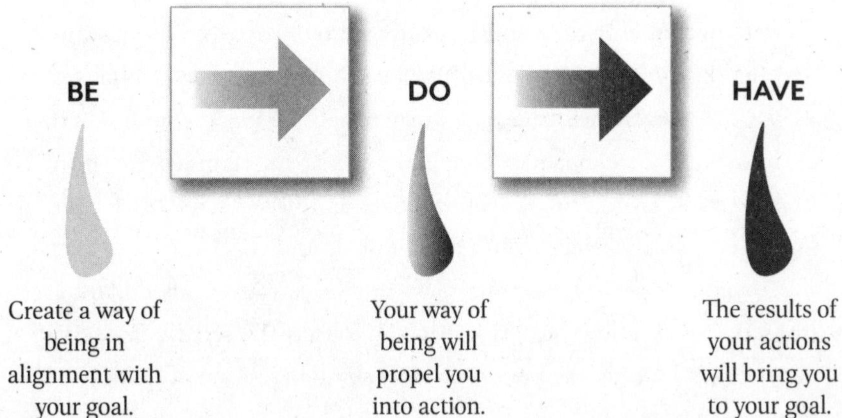
BE
DO
HAVE
Create a way of being in alignment with your goal.
Your way of being will propel you into action.
The results of your actions will bring you to your goal.

The Be, Do, Have model says that when we focus on living with an open heart, for example, we will take actions that a person with an open heart will take, and we will thereby attract other people and experiences who also align with open-hearted behavior.

The following Instagram caption was written by a woman named Sophia Esperanza on September 26, 2021. For years, Esperanza was an Instagram influencer and professional model, most notably known for being the face of Forever 21. Her feed was full of content with likes and views in the hundreds of thousands, representing the social media standard of "success." On that fall day, Sophia deleted almost all of her content in what seemed like a ceremony to cut the cords of attachment to all places where she (and everyone else) externalized her value and worth. The words she wrote beautifully capture the power of prioritizing her *being* and desired quality of life over *having* surface-level achievements and assets like followers and fame.

> It took just 30 minutes to erase 5 years of content and for a moment, I really enjoyed the thought of deleting my personal account entirely. I felt as if I had a mental bondage, duty to check in and responsibility to entertain. I say this to simply remind us of the impact social media

has on the mind, body, and soul. For some it may be such a small portion of your daily lives, you feel unaffected by its grasp. For most, it's nothing short of an addiction. Addiction to likes, comments, followers, views . . . I've even been to events where people are logging onto sites to see how 'well' someone's page is doing, that's sitting right next to them. Only to make silent remarks if they aren't up to their standards of performance. A real person, reduced to numbers and charts.

I want to remind everyone that your value transcends dollars. It transcends the followers staring back at you on the screen. It doesn't depend on a blue check. And it certainly shouldn't be a tool to measure your worth in this realm.

—@sophiaesperanza

Esperanza's post shows us how "having it all" doesn't automatically equate to happiness, satisfaction, or fulfillment. To me, it shows that Esperanza spent time doing her inner work, reflecting on her values, and aligning her behaviors and actions to those. Now, she's posting whatever she wants, even if they aren't what gets the most engagement—including her interests and passions like vegan activism and environmental sustainability. Those small, daily choices you make as a Content Creator are where you decide what your standards are for your own self-expression and freedom.

EMBODYING YOUR FREE AND CONFIDENT SELF

When you start remembering to come back to yourself and ask, "What do I truly want out of this?" and "What will I not allow myself to be influenced by?" you become more and more liberated from perceived pressures and boxes. We've all got our own battles to fight with the narratives in our head and those imposed upon us by society. But your practice of being in your own truth as a Content Creator is leadership. It's showing yourself and other people that you won't act in accordance with what's expected of you but rather with what you expect of yourself, coming from a place of compassionate self-acceptance and inner strength. The version of yourself that feels confident enough to embody this on a regular basis is inevitable—and it's only a matter of time until you feel more like them. That version of yourself is accepted in your community, making the kind of money that is a tool for your freedom, and is adored by your online community that receives value from you regularly. You're receiving just as much love and energy as you're giving. To step into that version of yourself even more quickly, take out your journal and answer these questions:

- How does the free and confident version of yourself act?
- What standards does this version of yourself enforce and uphold?
- What does this version of yourself not allow for in their world? What bullshit do they not play into online?
- What does this version of yourself believe about themself that allows them to show up freely and powerfully?
- How does this version of yourself feel?

Picture that version of yourself in your mind, right now.

- How do they look? What are they wearing?
- What emotion or energy does this version of you embody?
- How do you feel being in their presence?
- Who is in their tribe, supporting them?
- Where are they living? What's their environment like?
- What's their daily routine like?

Now—envision yourself as if you're actually that version of yourself. Feel what it's like to be this person. Allow the energy of that person to fill up your system from your head, all the way down to your toes. Remember this feeling—because this is just a *taste* of what it's like to truly live for yourself by embodying your values. When it comes to manifesting more of what you want and stepping into the more present and self-confident version of yourself, however, there's one part that we cannot bypass in the process of getting there: the darker, more shadowy energies at play. One of the best ways to get more of what you want is to address all of the belief systems, conditioning, dynamics, and unresolved emotional pain that keeps you in a holding pattern. The next section will teach you how to look at these darker, more negative energies in your social media energy field—including technology overwhelm, haters, trolls, critics, and even emotional trauma.

part two
part two
part two
part two

Protecting Yourself from the Dark Side of Social Media

five

Rewriting Your Social Media Narrative

On October 28, 2003, the history of connectivity changed when a group of students at Harvard University launched a website that displayed pictures of two women and prompted visitors to rank them against one another. The legend goes that, in addition to accruing thousands of hits in a few hours, Mark Zuckerberg's FaceMash also crashed the university servers. In February of 2004, after many apologies and some image rehab, the site was relaunched as a social media service instead of a hot-or-not clone, and thus was born The Facebook.

The abridged version of Facebook's history has been documented ad nauseum, but it runs parallel to another historical technological development: the widespread adoption of smartphones. The iPhone debuted in 2007, a mere year after Facebook—which had theretofore limited access to college students—made its service available to the public. The dovetailing of these events created a surge for both products: the smartphone allowed unfettered access to our social media feeds, which in turn meant we spent a lot of time on our smartphones.

Facebook immediately embraced a mobile-first mentality, focusing on simplicity, speed, and a smooth user experience with its app. The social media sites of the day were much slower to the mobile game. MySpace, for example, doubled down on the customizable profiles its users had loved. This was a miscalculation—while MySpace users *did* enjoy feeling like low-level programmers changing fonts and backgrounds with HTML, this was a computer-based and therefore stationary experience. Facebook, on the other hand, was in your pocket.

RIP TO BRB

The resulting boom came hard and fast. So amazed with our shiny devices, we had little in the way of forethought as the dopamine hits came over and over. As we developed an intimate relationship with our smartphones, there was an automatic shift in our relationship to the internet itself. Instead of living in the physical reality and sometimes being online, we now exist online and are sometimes logged off. We've stopped saying "brb" if we leave our keyboards because we've stopped leaving them. When we step away from our laptops, we still have our phones. Work emails come in at all hours. Text-message communication runs as an ongoing dialogue, replacing phone calls with their definitive beginnings and endpoints, and there's expectation around response time. We've created a world in which everything is not just instant but *constant*: always connected, plugged in, and online.

There's something intoxicating about this. You can message almost anyone, any time you want. You can be immediately notified when someone posts a new piece of content. You can consume very intimate details of your favorite Creators' personal lives. Twenty-four-hour immediate access can make it feel like everyone is just . . . available.

That stark, intense growth our society has experienced as a result has created high amounts of light-and-shadow aspects in the world we're all still learning how to deal with.

BE CAREFUL WHAT YOU LET IN YOUR HEAD

Your social media space is *your* home. *Your* little corner of the internet. *Your* personal platform to do and be exactly as you are. This space should be an environment of self-expression, authentic connection, and inspired action.

And yet—it's no secret to any of us that social media can have a dark edge to it. Just as there are light-and-dark polarities elsewhere in the world, social media is another manifestation of that same spectrum. Are there loads of opportunities, growth, impact, money, community, finding your voice, and purpose? Definitely. Is there also a high probability you'll encounter things like criticism, bullying, catfishing, fear of missing out, depression, anxiety, cancel culture, loneliness, digital addiction, and even digital warfare? Absolutely.

Remember FaceMash? By its nature, a site that interactively and algorithmically ranks women against one another without their consent is problematic, but perhaps the most concerning aspect of Zuckerberg's Facebook progenitor was its success. Every person who cast a vote knew they were violating inherent rights to privacy—not to mention dignity—but there was no shortage of people repeatedly clicking and casting votes.

From the very earliest stages of the internet, it's been apparent that bad actors and troublemakers will eschew compassion to garner attention. We'll cover trolls in greater detail in chapter eight, but for now it's enough to say that access is often enough to invite ire. Add anonymity, and you have an environment where assholes can take every opportunity to cause harm.

Let's go back to the idea of constant connection. As a Content Creator, you've probably felt that pressure to post, to share, to respond, to stay engaged—especially when your brand is connected to your business or income. Leaving comments on and open can be misinterpreted as a blank space for anyone to do or say whatever they want. The world of DMs, unsolicited opinions, dick pics, and emotional dumping can flood your inbox without a moment's notice. All of this can greatly affect your health and well-being if you don't have solid boundaries in place. In fact, this is one of the many reasons people avoid becoming Content Creators in the first place—because it can be . . . well, a lot to handle.

For most Content Creators, deleting your social media accounts isn't an option, so being your own best advocate for your well-being is the most supportive thing you can do to sustain a long-standing career as a Content Creator. In this chapter, you'll see how you can take some simple, intentional action steps to shift from resentfully tolerating social media to joyfully creating content on the medium to share your message.

PERFORM A SOCIAL MEDIA SCRUB

We're going to start with cleaning up your social media environment by cleaning it from the inside out and then focusing on making it fun, interactive, and inspiring. Just like the quote "We are the five people we spend the most time with," we also become the five Creators we consume the most content from. If you've felt stuck or stressed going online, it's time to clean up your space and clear out what's no longer serving you. Find someplace comfy, settle in, and let's go through the below steps!

Step 1: Unfollow or Unsubscribe from Accounts That Don't Feel like a "Hell Yes"

For this first step, think of it as Marie Kondo's KonMari method of organizing, which emphasizes decluttering and removing items that no longer resonate—and only keeping what "sparks joy." To apply Kondo's method to your social media, remove the *accounts* in your feed that don't "spark joy," to borrow Kondo's phrasing.

If you're following an account that does not leave you feeling inspired, educated, entertained, or supported in your journey, there's no need for it to take up space in your feed. When you follow accounts you no longer resonate with, feel guilty unfollowing, or are following for the "candy" but are left with no *nourishment*, spending hours a day on social media apps will always leave you feeling drained.

Practically speaking, unfollowing or unsubscribing might take you some time, especially if you are following hundreds or even thousands of accounts. Not only that, but many apps will flag you as a robot or potential spam account for unfollowing or following too many accounts at once, potentially leaving you banned from performing certain actions on the app altogether—eek! No one wants that. Spread this process out over the course of a week or two by doing a little each day. It will also feel far less overwhelming for you, too.

A few years ago, I walked one of my clients through their entire social media scrub, going through each person they followed, one by one. Some accounts felt easy for her to unfollow because she had no direct relationship with them, and it wouldn't have "meant" anything if those people found out. Another group of accounts required a bit of contemplation but no longer than a few seconds. A select group of people required some real processing around what it might mean to unfollow them:

- Would they take it personally?
- Would they unfollow her back?
- Would that hold any meaning for their future relationship?

The accounts that feel more difficult to make a decision about are often one of the following:

- Someone from your own industry whom you've admired but who ultimately distracts you from your own creativity
- A person with whom you've had a light or past relationship but whose content you don't necessarily want to consume anymore
- Someone with whom you've had a falling-out

Throughout this scrubbing process, my client was able to make some intentional decisions that felt right for her and she ultimately walked away feeling like there was a weight lifted off her shoulders and that there was no longer an energy trap keeping her stuck in consumption and comparison. And, of course, she started to enjoy being on social media a lot more, as it became a place of inspiration and fun.

Step 2: Mute Accounts You Want to Stay Connected to Without Consuming Their Content

Muting accounts is a strategic move, allowing you to stop consuming someone's regular updates and activity without them knowing. You may want to stay in contact and connection, or perhaps you're not ready to have a conversation about a public unfollow. That's perfectly fine! Muting is great for maybe an ex-boyfriend or your best friend from college, where you have history and a connection but don't feel the need to see every post and story they make. Perhaps you follow a business or influencer to remind yourself to go back and buy products they advertise, but you don't want to have their posts popping up on your feed midday when you're trying to minimize spending. All good—and quite smart, in fact.

Many of the business-owner clients I've had have found it particularly helpful to mute their colleagues and the "leading voices" in their particular space. As much as it can be great to be aware of what some of the top voices are saying, an overwhelming number of my clients have reported that the juice isn't worth the squeeze when it comes to staying connected to their own authentic voice. Creators often follow other Creators in their industry, and as amazing as it is to connect and collaborate, it can make it difficult to feel like your mind is clear from all the noise and messages everyone else is saying when you go to create your own content. In fact, it may even create an experience that highlights your downfalls or how you lack in comparison to others—which sits on this pretty blurred line between "growth-inducing" and "triggering." Unfollowing or muting people is a great move if you feel like you have to repeatedly face feelings of comparison, inadequacy, or even just overwhelm from other people who affect your ability to create content.

Step 3. Diversify Your Feed for Education and Growth

One of the largest benefits of social media is being able to essentially receive a passive education through short-form content on a daily basis. TikTok doesn't necessarily replace formal education, but how much have you learned from finding accounts entirely outside of your niche that shared educational content you were interested in? A fantastic way to take advantage of the learning you can receive from online Creators is to follow people who don't fit within your usual echo chamber of accounts and viewpoints.

An echo chamber is this experience of seeing a certain type of message or content so regularly in our feed that it feels like the entirety of reality. However, that echo chamber is just mirroring back to you more of what you want to see—the same message that sounds familiar and generally falls within your own biases and belief systems. You could be in a conspiracy-theory echo chamber, or a lipstick echo chamber, or a CrossFit echo chamber, or a gentle-parenting echo chamber. An echo chamber is essentially one big confirmation bias: you believe the world is a particular way because that's what you're consuming on a daily basis. In the Netflix documentary *The Social Dilemma,* it was shown that these kinds of algorithms can go as far as to affect elections, voting, and other geopolitical and social movements, deepening people into belief systems that continue to confirm their own biases. This is the extreme end of this problem.

Of course, it's completely up to you whose content you want to be consuming every day, but it's useful to expand your sense of how the lived experiences of other people shape their perspectives. If someone doesn't look like you (e.g., race, gender identity, religion, industry, niche) or have the same lived experiences as you do, it will help to open up your world and bring their new ideas and ways of thinking into your reality. If you don't do this intentionally, the algorithm will unfortunately keep bringing you more of the same.

Step 4: Nourish Yourself by Interacting with Accounts That Feel Light and Playful

The reason the phrase "We are the five people we spend the most time with" rings so true for so many people is because we don't generally experience much diversity of thought outside of those people closest to us. Even if you don't believe you are easily influenced, our subconscious minds are designed to constantly take in information to develop our overall worldview and individual perspective. Similarly, your reality is heavily influenced by the people you follow the most regularly.

After recommitting to the accounts or Creators you *didn't* scrub out and intentionally choosing new accounts to follow—go enjoy 'em! These are the people you've decided will be most supportive to your growth, inspiration, education, or entertainment for your next season. This should help you feel a type of inspiration and support that allows your social media home to actually make you feel like you can sit back and relax. Doing this helps you have a healthier, more functional relationship with the social media platforms you're on. Go enjoy those TikTok dance videos or acting skits. Listen to structured and thought-provoking interviews on a new podcast you found or simply enjoy puppy videos!

If you're a Content Creator, think of yourself like a digital athlete—and social media is your playing field. If you're going to perform well, stay highly creative on the regular, and engage with a growing audience, you'll need to make sure you're feeding yourself with proper nutrients (aka content that supports and fuels you). The content you consume can affect your physical body, thoughts, beliefs, emotions, and so much more. If what you're consuming isn't helping you feel better, it's time to reevaluate your consumption and improve your relationship to social media.

A social media scrub can do wonders for your time online. It can become a time where you enjoy seeing the content you have chosen to absorb, a time to become inspired and get that little hit of inspiration to keep you feeling engaged and excited about being a Content Creator! Put the book down if you have to, but if you're ready, go ahead and start the scrub now—or mark some time in your calendar to complete it this week.

WHY CONTENT CREATORS NEED BOUNDARIES–AND HOW TO SET THEM

Cleaning up your social media environment is going to feel like you just got your hair done or did a deep clean of your house—fresh, freeing, and just a little better than before. Continuing down this same path of creating a satisfying and freeing space for yourself online, the next step is to talk about your boundaries—those invisible agreements that state what you are and aren't available for in your life.

Typically, boundaries are spoken about as they relate to the actions or behaviors you won't tolerate from other people (e.g., "I will not be spoken to that way"), but you can also have boundaries with yourself (e.g., "I will not speak to myself that way"). Having clear, strong boundaries allows you to deeply protect your energy, your peace, and your mental and emotional state from anything that is not preferable to experience—and, at the most extreme end of the spectrum, anything that is not psychologically safe for you to experience. Forming and setting personal boundaries is a skill that allows you to create an environment where you can thrive and minimizes situations that may negatively impact your health and well-being. Boundaries also support you in cultivating feelings of self-trust—you've got your own back because you advocate for your own needs and all the areas you may want to set boundaries in.

One of my stronger boundaries is that I will block anyone who blatantly disrespects me on my feed or in my DMs. This doesn't mean I block every person who disagrees with me or every person who is petty, snarky, or rude—but it does mean that any person who actively disrespects me or other people I care about gets blocked. If this were real life, I simply would not allow any of those types of people to enter my home or physical space—so enforcing that same standard in my social media world only makes sense.

Your most important relationships on social media are with the platform, with your audience, and with yourself. Like any relationship, setting up clear expectations and creating personal agreements about what is and isn't okay in the space is how you teach people how to treat you. Not every audience member will automatically know that you hate getting inquiries in your DMs and would prefer email, for example. Of course, there are plenty of "golden rule"–type expectations we may expect all human beings to just know and abide by. But still—everyone has different perspectives of what is and isn't okay, especially when there can be a sense of entitlement and access woven into aspects of the fabric of social media.

It's important to be clear and direct about what your expectations are with your audience members. This way, you can maintain as much integrity and respect as possible. It's as simple as having these expectations publicly visible for everyone to see. Perhaps you have a highlight with disclaimers, boundaries, and expectations. Maybe you post a reminder every once in a while about what your relationship to messenger communication is like and your overall availability with social media.

Other-Centric Boundaries Around Communication and Availability

Your time and energy are precious resources that you get to manage however you see fit to help you have the most supportive life you can. Boundaries you set around how you communicate with people online and how available you are for certain conversations are important to set, even if it's just for your own awareness. If you're a person who loves to engage with people in your community on a daily basis and keep multiple conversations going, you may need to be more explicit in saying which kinds of conversations you aren't available to have in your DMs. If you're a person who does not have the bandwidth to DM people at all, acknowledge that so people know how to engage with you. If the default assumption is "always available," we have to work to let other people know what we are and aren't available for. One of my personal-favorite boundaries I set for myself was deciding to engage with people when I felt like my cup was full rather than from a place of being drained. My attention goes to my inner circle the most, and then paying clients, and then to outer circles and potential clients, and then to my community members who follow me. Not everyone is entitled to my energy, and I am not obligated to respond to every message that comes into my inbox—especially with the sheer volume of messages there are. In fact, my brain has created a rather intelligent filtration system where I trust my own energy to determine what I do and don't respond to. It's a combination of the type of message and how much energy I have that day. I love connecting with people and being a beacon of support, but I can't lose sleep or lose energy over not getting back to everyone. The moment I internally released any guilt I had around that, the more I freed myself up to become even more efficient and peaceful than I was prior.

Self-Centric Boundaries Around Emotional Labor

There will be social media activities that require a lot of emotional labor from you, and that's more than okay. You do not have to engage in conversations if you're sensing that it's affecting your health and well-being. Ask yourself: What feels like a "hell no" in my body? What actions or activities feel like I'm experiencing diminishing returns on my efforts?

A *hard boundary* around your social media actions may sound like this:

"It is stressing me out far too much to expect myself to respond to every message and guilt myself when I don't. I'm going to free myself from that expectation for my own well-being."

Flexible boundaries are strong preferences you stand for that have a few exceptions, like emergencies or time-sensitive issues. They may sound like this:

"I usually don't respond to DMs over the weekends, but my cup feels full today, so I'm going to spend some time responding! In fact—it could free up my time another day this week when I'm feeling more tired."

Mutual agreements are boundaries around behavior and processes that prioritize both parties (you and your audience) fairly equally. They could sound like this:

"If you repost my work to your page, it feels important for me to be tagged. Is that something you can agree to?"

English fiction author Alexis Hall (@quicunquevult) made a point to clearly state his boundaries at the bottom of multiple Instagram posts in a row. The boundary states:

> A note: Something I've noticed lately is that some people seem to be treating my social media not as my social media but a sort of generic space where they can act however they like. The thing is, that is not the case. You are in my house—where you are very welcome—talking directly to me. Please don't misunderstand, I love interacting with readers, I'm grateful beyond measure for your support of my work, and I want you to be comfortable. But I am also a person. If you treat me like a punching bag, complain about aspects of the publishing process beyond my control, or willfully transgress my boundaries your comment will be removed.

To set your emotional-labor boundaries for your audience to know how to interact with you, set clear expectations in some section of your profile. "If you communicate with me in this way, I won't hesitate to block you immediately" is a great way to communicate a boundary with your audience. Review chapter eight for more information on writing disclaimers and setting clear expectations with your audience.

Self-Centric Boundaries Around Technology and Content Consumption

My best friend, Ashley, and her family take a summer boating trip to Lake Havasu every year, and I was invited to go with them in June 2018. The temperature was close to ninety-five degrees, and her mom recommended we just leave our phones in the car—first, they could overheat, and second, there wasn't service out on the lake anyway. Once we boated over to the cove and set up our tents and beach chairs, I sank into the chair and began to notice something.

Sky.

Mountain.

Water.

Sand.

My brain focused on just four inputs—not counting the twenty or so other people in Ashley's family at the cove with us. I could feel the sensation of inflammation in my brain decreasing. The muscles behind my eyes could finally relax. Four inputs—that's it. All nature and nothing else for ten hours.

I realized that the energy consumption of staring at my phone and laptop for hours a day was the main source of my low energy and stress. By the end of the day, my body and cells felt completely revitalized. Sure, the sun and play helped. But I've had plenty of days scrolling through my phone by the pool, and they didn't even come close to how peaceful I felt with the limited inputs, blue light, stimulation, and information consumption that came as a result of not having my phone for one whole day.

Our relationships with our phones and scrolling through social media platforms are our personal responsibility to navigate. Unfortunately, we are fighting against algorithms that are designed to keep you addicted to scrolling and usage. I'm not ashamed to admit that breaking the habit of constant scrolling is still a challenge for me, even now. Sure, having social events where I feel fully present or being on vacation in places that don't have service or Wi-Fi helps with this. Some forced social media detoxes can be made easier through accountability and doing it with other people. But I'm still not perfect. If you've ever trained a dog, you know that it's constant upkeep to maintain the skills and behaviors you worked hard to get them to unlearn—and it's the same with scrolling. The more we unconsciously scroll, the deeper the neural pathways will groove in our brain and become automatic. This is why it's so challenging to truly end our scrolling habits. And that's why it's helpful to approach your own social and tech detoxes and habits in a way that's realistic.

Technology and Social Media Detoxes

There are moments where I catch myself deep in a scroll hole—finding it difficult to rip myself away from the screen, knowing that being in that loop creates a kind of low-level anxiety that is just tolerable enough to keep going.

Those moments are when I remember how important it is to consistently practice actively interrupting that pattern with some version of a social media detox. It might feel impossible or daunting to fully unplug from the online world altogether, so the options for taking a break (listed below) are helpful to figure out how to make this task realistic and doable for yourself. Rather than being all or nothing, can you fully commit to taking the afternoon off and logging out? Or going offline while you finish an important task? Or even just taking a break from creating? The key is to create options for yourself that live within the spectrum between "all" and "nothing." Rather than saying, "I'm going to delete every social media app and lock my phone in a timed lockbox all weekend!" try one of these more flexible approaches:

- **Feed-post break.** Set a time frame (rigid or loose) for how long you're going to stop posting on your feed. It may sound silly, but as a Content Creator, creating YouTube videos, recording podcasts, or writing Instagram posts can feel far more daunting than shooting out a quick email to your list or making an easy TikTok in the moment. Face it: some types of content just feel more serious and require more effort than others. Let some of the more daunting formats take a back seat and watch your energy free up!
- **Content creation break.** Allow yourself to keep the apps and continue to consume, but stop content creation for a period of time. This is best for you if you find yourself faced with complete resistance to writing, filming, or recording. That resistance is a great sign to stop forcing it and let go of that grip for a while. You won't become irrelevant, and your algorithm will be fine. Nothing is going to break or blow up. When you rest and rejuvenate, you'll have the space to feel that same frictionless flow with your content when you arrive back.
- **Log out for a bit.** Any time you're feeling that itch to feel less anxious, stressed, or plugged into the internet, log out of your accounts for a while. Do this to complete a project or to enjoy the weekend without looking at your phone.

> "I dare you . . . Visibility these days seems to somehow equate to success. Do not be afraid to disappear—from it, from us—for a while, and see what comes to you in the silence."
>
> MICHAELA COEL

THE AGREEMENTS YOU MAKE WITH YOURSELF

Now that we've examined your relationship with boundaries in detail and have learned some approaches to social media detoxing, let's come up with some personal agreements for you to align how you want to feel with a clear standard for how you operate online. An agreement is a personal standard you decide on regarding what you will and won't do. Think of agreements like an internal set of behaviors, mindsets, and intentions all wrapped up into a system that helps you feel free and expressed. These can encompass some of the boundaries and approaches we've already discussed in this chapter—but tailored to you and your own needs. Having predetermined agreements that can expand and evolve with you will help being online feel more satisfying and empowering because you're essentially committing to live in accordance with your values.

To help you come up with agreements, I've created an exercise for you to build them in a way that helps you think more deeply about how you can honor your needs and desires as a Content Creator. The exercise is called "Building a Personal Truth Declaration." For you to feel the most satisfied, joyful, respected, and supported as a Content Creator, what agreements do you need to set? The box below will walk you through an example of what a personal truth declaration could look like. You can also head to followedbook.io to write in the accompanying digital journaling space and build your own Personal Truth Declaration there. Consider writing a statement for each of the below areas:

- Frequency and cadence of posting
- Responding to messages and availability
- Consuming content and time spent online
- Emotional labor and energy expended for others online

Here is an example of what your Personal Truth Declaration can look like, incorporating your boundaries and the relationship you want to have with the different aspects and audiences of your social media platforms:

MY PERSONAL TRUTH DECLARATION

I vow to honor my sensitivity and need for space from social media by logging off on the weekends and limiting comments on certain posts.

I vow to clearly communicate my important boundaries with my audience, especially those that protect my mental and emotional well-being.

At this time in my life, I can see myself posting on my feed once a week, but I feel aligned with sending every new follower a welcome DM to initiate and build personal relationships.

I will set aside one hour each afternoon to engage with my community in the comments section, through messages, and in the comments section of other people's content.

I will not teach what I don't feel fully embodied in just yet—especially if there's a health, financial, or mental-health component I know could be harmful. I will, however, teach what I'm clear I know "enough" of to do no harm. Posting will better help me teach what I do know.

I will not take on sponsorships, brand deals, or partnerships that are not in alignment with my values. I will take time to evaluate these and act once I have clarity. There will always be opportunities, and I choose to value my reputation and community more than I value monetary gain.

I will not respond to every DM conversation to maintain my energy for paying clients, friends, family members, and myself. This will allow me to show up more engaged and magnetize the right people for me.

If I feel triggered, I will not respond instantly. I will walk away from the platform and take as much time as I need before choosing to respond, engage, or take action.

I will allow myself to unfollow, unsubscribe, mute, or block anyone I desire without explanation.

I will allow myself to post less on social media while I grow into the discipline and practice of writing my book. It's an edge to step away from the "safety" of the short-form daily content I've become used to and use that energy for a long-form book that won't be finished for many months.

I will allow myself to pivot industries or deepen my niche if I feel called to go down that path. I will take the time to reflect and make conscious choices, to enjoy exploring, and to allow myself to feel the excitement fully.

six

The Link Between Trauma and Social Media

This can't be happening.

Wait, how *is this even happening?*

Shocked and frightened, I couldn't believe what was unfolding before my eyes.

I refreshed my Twitter feed every twenty minutes and saw a steady influx of over two hundred new tweets and retweets. Comments on previous threads were being added by the minute; new threads were growing.

People wrote:

"She shouldn't be allowed on the internet."

"Don't ever give your money to this woman."

"People like her are the reason why we have eating disorders."

And all I wanted was to crawl into a hole and die.

In a continuous thread of harsh critiques, my character and morals were called into question and exposed for the world to discuss. Regardless of how much it hurt me, I couldn't pull myself away from my phone to stop reading the comments. Some people may have had the strength to shrug it off as "just social media; it comes with the territory." Not me—not then. Watching hundreds of people dissect my actions felt like watching a train crash unfolding in slow motion—only *this* train was my life and reputation. I couldn't peel my eyes away, and I couldn't avoid the truth any longer.

I got canceled.

Ashamed and embarrassed by the onslaught of criticism, I slumped deeper into my massive beanbag in the corner of my LA apartment. My body ached with shame—I sobbed uncontrollably and couldn't stop. I *had* to consider how probable it was that I did, in fact, go wrong somewhere, and maybe they were right. I had a very public platform, complete with power, influence, and responsibility. There was no hiding from my mistakes—but that didn't make it any less emotionally overwhelming.

A tidal wave of fear engulfed me as my threat-protection system activated. I seemed to cycle through all the trauma responses:

- *Fuck these assholes!* (Fight)
- *I'm gonna delete my YouTube channel.* (Flight)
- *I don't know what to do.* (Freeze)
- *I need to respond to all of these!* (Fawn)

As the cancellation continued to unfold, one particularly damaging sentence swirled around in my mind:

"Scamanda is trying to profit off vulnerable women with eating disorders."

I spiraled. "*Oh my fucking fuck.* How could something *so innocent* get interpreted as such an appalling action?!" How was I going to recover from an accusation that was so damaging?

Here was the deal. I grew my social media audience at a very young age, and people mostly followed me for my fitness, nutrition, and bodybuilding-competition content. At the time (2017), there were some infrequent posts from Content Creators in the industry about the negative effects of diet culture and extreme fat loss and the intrinsic link between the competition world and disordered eating. Nowadays, the fitness industry has evolved to heavily include conversations about a person's relationship with food. In fact, entire subniches have been created as a result of some of the problematic issues that diet culture has activated for so many people, like root-cause healing for relationships with food through trauma healing. But back then, I hadn't yet unpacked the privileges I held, nor did I have the education or training to understand what was necessary medical treatment for those with eating disorders and more severe challenges with food, body image, and mental health. Pair this lack of awareness with marketing, and it was all a recipe for potential harm.

A few weeks prior to this barrage of hate, I decided to join forces with a health-coach friend of mine who wanted to cohost a webinar on "Healing Your Relationship with Food." At the time, I thought this was a great idea to help people understand themselves more deeply—but as aforementioned, that topic wasn't yet popular or normalized like it is now. In hindsight, though, I recognize that some of the language used to promote that webinar was problematic and unattuned to the tender vulnerabilities of those who may be in need of medical attention or may require a more nuanced approach to healing their relationship with food.

Fast-forward to the marketing-campaign release and subsequent Twitter fiasco, and I found myself stunned and confused, processing how we could've possibly gone wrong. *This guy I collaborated with seemed smart—but should I have vetted him further? Is this on him? Do I blame him? They're saying I should never have gotten involved with that "slime ball." Is my judgment off? What's* wrong *with me? How could I be so stupid? Shit shit shit. What did I do?*

Wait, did I even do anything? Is this that *bad?* I had many doubts and questions but very little certainty on how to move forward.

Over the next few days, my body reacted by slowly shutting down. I completely lost my appetite and could barely sleep. Forget important work-related activities like marketing and operating my business—my life had whittled down to incessantly checking my phone. Unsurprisingly, the constant checking didn't actually provide me any relief—instead, I stayed hyperaware of all the comments people were saying, keeping me wired and on edge. I felt a painful pang with each new tweet that I saw. Everyone and everything felt like a potential threat. I felt like a dog backed into a corner, scared and helpless—yet still on the lookout and ready to attack. Fear built at a rapid rate inside me, anchoring these memories as reference points for what I never wanted to happen again. It felt like I was in a never-ending nightmare.

In the coming days, walls built around my heart. I closed myself off from the world, protected myself in a cocoon, and hardened. I thought the world would simply be better off if I didn't exist. Shame anchored in my body, reinforcing the feeling that Twitter and YouTube were no longer safe. I wasn't sure I would ever be able to post a YouTube video again. Perhaps I could, but if I did, I'd have to start a new channel rather than resurrect my old one.

I felt the temptation to justify and explain what I'd meant, for them to see my side of things, to convince them of my innocence—but any effort I made to clear things up seemed pointless. "Being defensive only proves you did something wrong," they'd say. *How is anyone to respond to something like this, then?* I wondered. In the following weeks and months, I had entire hate Instagram accounts made about me that screenshotted my every move and used it as ammunition for people to decide that my character was, in fact, immoral. I even had hate videos and hate podcasts made about me.

The experience was emotionally overwhelming and psychologically damaging, leaving an impact—or what we now know as *trauma*.

THE LINK BETWEEN TRAUMA AND SOCIAL MEDIA

> "When a person is exposed to overwhelming stress, threat or injury, they develop a procedural memory. Trauma occurs when these implicit procedures are not neutralized. The failure to restore homeostasis is at the basis for the maladaptive and debilitating symptoms of trauma."
>
> PETER A. LEVINE

I'm well aware that death, abuse, war, and other life-threatening and catastrophic situations are far worse and that getting yelled at, called out, or canceled on social media may seem trivial. But the emotional spiral I experienced—similar to what many other Creators have felt on varying levels—left such an impact on my sense of emotional safety online. There are Content Creators who receive daily attacks, sometimes ones even suggesting that they should go kill themselves or that they are too fat or ugly to deserve to live. The veil between the in-person world and social media world has lifted, and the link between the two is intrinsic and deeply connected, forever. What happens on social media can have very real, long-lasting consequences on people that impact and affect their personal and professional lives.

In choosing to dive into social media to garner the rewards and benefits available to you, it's very helpful to understand what else you might have to navigate mentally, emotionally, and spiritually by doing so. While this isn't a book about trauma or healing trauma, it will be absolutely important for you to understand the basics of how your trauma from the past or the trauma you've endured as a result of social media could be impacting your experience as a Content Creator. It would be a missed opportunity to not at least touch upon key concepts surrounding trauma that can affect the ability for someone to be the best Content Creator they can be. I have had clients who I've referred to therapists because they needed therapeutic support, and it's imperative that people get this kind of support if they need it.

The fifth edition of the *Diagnostic and Statistical Manual of Mental Disorders* (DSM-5) defines trauma as including "actual or threatened death, serious injury, or sexual violence." Another definition by Dr. Peter Levine, founder of Somatic Experiencing®, says trauma is "when a person is exposed to overwhelming stress, threat or injury" and develops "a procedural memory" of that experience. On the Somatic Experiencing website, it is also mentioned that "the traumatic event isn't what causes long-lasting trauma, it is the overwhelming trapped response to the perceived life-threat that is causing an imbalanced nervous system." Mastin Kipp, transformational coach and best-selling author known for his work studying trauma, said in his Trauma-Informed Coaching Certification, "Trauma is an experience of threat, disconnection, isolation or immobilization that results in physical/emotional injuries that dysregulate the optimal function of one's body, emotions, brain, spirit or health."

In each of these definitions, there are two core components that make an experience traumatic:

- Overwhelming stress beyond the capacity of the individual's nervous system—whether that's a physical threat of death or perceived emotional threat
- Physiological or psychological stuckness, negatively impacting one's well-being

In recent years (specifically with the rise of "Insta-therapy" and pop psychology), millions more humans have learned and discovered what trauma is. This awareness and discovery is amazing, allowing people to receive support, heal, and become thriving humans. However, when it comes to content online, there is the possibility for a complex concept such as trauma to become a buzzword or buzz concept, accompanied with various and possibly distorted definitions and interpretations that may not adequately represent it.

For the purposes of this book, it's important to understand the distinction between "capital-T trauma" and "lowercase-t trauma." The purpose of the distinction is not to minimize or dismiss the impact of any events you've experienced as traumatic but to ensure that there are adequate protections in place for the victims and survivors with a requirement for higher treatment and care.

Major catastrophic events like war, abuse, natural disasters, violence, or sexual assault are considered capital-T trauma. Without proper treatment and support, traumatic events like these can *severely* impact an individual's quality of life and ability to thrive. These events may require professional medical treatment in the long term to minimize any ongoing symptoms of trauma.

Lowercase-t traumas are events and experiences that don't land with the same weight as their counterparts. Lowercase-t traumas aren't instances of assault or abuse; they're very often cumulative instead of acute. And they can be easily overlooked or even forgotten. But the body remembers and records experiences as impactful. These could include invasive medical procedures, racial discrimination, or even giving birth.[5]

Not every stressful or uncomfortable experience is going to lead to trauma anchoring in the body. Sometimes, people just suffer, experience distress, and are affected by that. But that isn't always trauma.

Getting laid off from your job during an economic recession and then experiencing financial hardship and loss can result in trauma symptoms. Going through an unexpected divorce with emotional, psychological, reputational, or financial damage can result in trauma symptoms. Having major friendship breakdowns and rebuilding your social life from scratch can be traumatic. Being harassed and having to justify your existence as a queer, trans, non-binary, or other marginalized person can be traumatic. Losing a year of your life recovering from adrenal fatigue or burnout after many bodybuilding competitions and losing followers and business as a result can be traumatic. If a situation has long-lasting effects that live in your body and arise when similar situations arise—that's trauma.

In these traumatic situations, without a way to repair itself, the body experiences a sense of stuckness. This presents as both psychological stuckness (e.g., anxiety, depression, PTSD, addiction, rage, insomnia, paranoia, dissociation, hypervigilance, shutdown) and physiological stuckness (e.g., IBS or gut issues, heart problems, inflammation, chronic pain, neurological issues, respiratory distress, and other breakdown of vital tissues and organs).

After you experience trauma, the imprint left on your body can affect your behavior. Unresolved trauma may mean you experience behavior patterns including (but not limited to):

- Controlling, hypervigilance, perfectionism, or micromanaging life to feel safe and minimize the potential for getting hurt again
- Agreeing to the status quo or minimizing and dimming yourself to keep the peace to avoid scenarios of feeling like a burden, too much, or not enough when you're authentically expressing yourself
- Feelings of emptiness, numbness, disconnection, and "leaving your body," more commonly known as dissociation
- Lashing out at others in rage or anger due to increased feelings of anxiety
- Seeking distraction or escape through different vehicles like food, alcohol, television, or drugs

> If you look at that list and suspect there may be a deeper issue you need to look at or feel like you're connecting some dots, put this book down and seek some professional support. We'll be here for you when you're ready.

The Wounds Left Behind

If *trauma* is the event or experience that happened, the *wound* is the psychological or emotional hurt and impact left behind.

Think of emotional wounds like physical cuts that can not only still be tender years later but can also leave the body riddled with scar tissue and become reminders of the pain and suffering from the event. Once someone has a wound, it can leave them feeling vulnerable, scared, and stuck. If a situation ever triggers you, chances are there is an underlying wound. Being triggered is when you have a substantially larger emotional response or reaction than that which a situation seems to warrant.[6] Our bodies store their responses to traumatic moments and seek to prevent those circumstances from recurring. As a survival mechanism, this is an elegant evolutionary response; as a lived experience, however, the hypervigilance can be exhausting. It can also prime us to interpret any remotely similar situation as dangerous, deepening the neural grooves of the trauma loop.

Contrary to popular proverbs, time itself doesn't heal all wounds (if only it were that easy!). But time with therapeutic modalities, safe relationships, and new safe experiences that help you move forward can all support in diluting the intensity of the wound. The good news is that humans have an innate ability to get unstuck, heal from trauma, and learn how to thrive again. While many people might turn to traditional talk therapy as they begin their healing journey, other modalities have often been found to be more effective when it comes to trauma. Somatic therapy, Eye Movement Desensitization and Reprocessing (EMDR), Internal Family Systems, and breathwork can often feel more effective because they allow the nervous system to gradually reestablish what feels safe in the body within the context of a safe relationship. EMDR in particular has been well supported in randomized research trials and meta-analyses and has even been endorsed by the World Health Organization, International Society for Traumatic Stress Studies, Department of Veterans Affairs, and the American Psychiatric Association.[7]

If you are seeking out therapeutic support, definitely take the time to look for a therapeutic modality that feels like a good fit to you—you may have to try a few different styles before you find the one that best works for you. You may need a focus on a particular modality, or perhaps a combination approach might be more effective. You might start out loving talk therapy but then find that you are drawn to somatic therapy, and that's okay. Your needs may change over time.

Wounding from our childhood is not necessarily any different than wounding that happens in adolescence or adulthood, but due to the cognitive functioning and abilities of the brain during our childhood, those traumas may leave more of a lasting impact. Children cannot comprehend that their parents are also dealing with their own traumas or wounding, and they don't always have the ability to use their thinking minds to logically process and understand a situation. Nor do children have the ability to fully regulate themselves or meet their own needs. In this way, childhood wounds can become embedded in one's psyche and color the lens through which we see the world.

Some of the most common wounds are:

- **Fear of abandonment.** This usually happens in childhood where a parental figure, physically or emotionally, leaves once or repeatedly, instilling a lack of safety and a fear that the child may be abandoned again. It can also happen as an adult if—for example—a long-term partner suddenly leaves unexpectedly without notice and contact. On social media, this wound may show up as a Content Creator putting off making a brand pivot due to an underlying fear of losing followers.

- **Fear of rejection.** When someone experiences rejection at an individual or group level, it can have a lasting impact. It may leave the person afraid of being authentic or vulnerable because they are scared of the possibility of experiencing rejection or that level of pain again. This could look like hiding mistakes or parts of yourself you've been rejected for in the past from your social media audience.
- **Difficulty trusting others.** There are many situations that may lead to a struggle with trusting others. This usually occurs when someone has experienced betrayal or uncertainty within relationships, and then there is a struggle to trust the words or actions of those closest to them. You might notice this showing up if you are very careful about what you say online, don't feel safe discussing or disclosing certain parts of yourself, or feel the need to keep your audience at a distance.
- **Fear of the unknown.** If you have experienced uncertainty and unpredictability, it may create a wound of fearing the unknown. This might originate from growing up with an unpredictable parent, mental illness, poverty, or general instability. On its surface, this wound may look like someone who is overly controlling or demanding, yet, underneath it all, someone filled with crippling fear and a desire to avoid uncertainty at all costs. This could manifest as tracking your follower count regularly, setting number goals with your engagement and following size, or becoming stuck, frozen, or anxious around doing something new online.
- **People-pleasing.** This is a wound very close to my heart. The people-pleasing wound leaves someone focused on making other people happy, even if it's to their own detriment, in order to keep the peace. This can come from somehow perceiving that one's own

needs, desires, authentic expression, or existence is a burden to others. If you struggle to set and enforce boundaries online or think often about making content for other people without making sure you're making it in a way that serves you, you may be struggling with this wound.

- **Perfectionism.** Perfectionism stems from the fear of being seen as imperfect, wrong, or not good enough as you are. The deep need to prove yourself to others (e.g., your parents, your teachers, the world) may appear as only sharing content you deem "good enough," not taking risks or stepping outside your comfort zone, and feeling an overwhelming sense of pressure to perform in a certain way. To prevent facing that fear, you might find yourself only posting content you've spent a lot of time "perfecting" or becoming stressed if you feel you've made a mistake in your content.
- **Fear of failure and fear of success.** Failure (or any standard deemed as less than winning) might not have been acceptable growing up. There might have been a loss of love, abuse, or neglect as a result of failing or not living up to certain expectations. Fear of success, on the other hand, is the fear of responsibility overwhelm and uncertainty around whether or not you have the emotional resilience to handle it all. Oftentimes, people can have an intertwined fear of success *and* failure—like a fear of both growing an audience and of not living up to people's expectations of you.

Please note: just because you experience these types of events, circumstances, experiences, or relationships does not mean you have a wound.

The full conversation about psychological safety is beyond the scope of this book, but it's imperative to touch upon as you're navigating through potentially impactful experiences that shape your life and potential to thrive as a human. If you've experienced intense situations like getting canceled, being cyberbullied, having lies made up about you that affected your reputation, or feeling violated in relationships with strangers who interact with your page, consider receiving therapeutic support. At that point, the impact these events may have had on you goes far beyond social media and has extended into your real, lived experience. And in order for you to feel safe in your social media spaces again, there is healing to do.

The fear you may feel, the walls you have up, the way you wear a metaphorical mask so as not to ever-so-vulnerably expose the "real" you—those are all highly intelligent ways your body protects you from potential harm. You might not even realize that you are behaving in these ways. But your body is doing what it perceives as best in order to keep you safe: setting boundaries, avoiding potentially risky situations, and maintaining distance from that which could be damaging. A little self-compassion and grace can go a long way here, too—we're all just doing our best to move forward and keep surviving.

seven

Embracing Your Social Media Shadow

For the first few years of being a Content Creator, I never discussed my political views with my audience. At the time, it wasn't considered necessary (or even encouraged) for influencers or nonpolitical figures to discuss any beliefs or views outside of their industries. But as major sociopolitical events went down from early 2020 onward, the culture of keeping your politics off your platform changed. Creators, brands, and businesses everywhere were asked to be transparent about their stances so consumers could make informed choices about who to support and where to spend their money. When it became apparent that it was time to inform my audience where I stood, I was terrified to share a truth I'd carried around but was terrified to admit: I was twenty-seven years old and had never voted in an election.

Before finally admitting this to my audience, I first had to admit to myself that avoiding using my voice, privilege, social status, and voting power was a part of me I felt *ashamed* of. It was extremely challenging to face this part of myself that I'd been avoiding for most of my young adulthood. I finally decided to post an IGTV video outlining my experience of why I'd never voted—a combination of privilege, avoidance of human suffering, keeping my head in the sand, and a general lack of dinner-table conversations about politics growing up. At that moment of facing my self-judgment and fear of being judged, I brought my *social media shadow* into the *light.*

WHAT IS THE SHADOW–AND WHAT DOES IT HAVE TO DO WITH BEING A CONTENT CREATOR?

In Jungian psychology, the *shadow* is defined as everything in the psyche that a person is not fully conscious or aware of. Think of the shadow as the aspects of the self that the conscious ego does not identify within itself—as those parts have been repressed, suppressed, rejected, shamed, or guilted.

For example: so many people who grew up in conservative or religious homes have been told that their sexuality or sexual expression was sinful, wrong, or unholy. In order to survive in that kind of environment, many of these people unconsciously tuck their connection to their sexual expression away in a little corner in the attic of their psyche. This type of action can result in a belief that you simply aren't a sexual person—or any other characteristic that would've normally felt very natural to you, had you not been conditioned to *reject* it.

Whatever qualities are praised and rewarded are the qualities that we feel emotionally safe expressing. With trauma and traumatic experiences, the parts of ourselves that get rejected, shamed, judged, or criticized by others will fragment away from our personality and into our shadow. The parts that remain are what we receive validation and love for and in turn become deeply ingrained in our minds as what our personality is. Think of it this way: there is no conscious without the unconscious, no light without dark.

WHAT IS SHADOW WORK?

Shadow work is an inner-healing practice that includes intentionally putting in effort to go up into that attic where the dark, unconscious parts of your psyche live—and find out exactly what is there in order to bring it back down to the living room of your conscious awareness, clean it up, and integrate it into your self-image. This can be done through journaling and self-reflection questions that are ultimately focused around one question:

What do I not want to see?

In my story of sharing my experience with voting, I could have easily kept hiding from myself and other people, just pretending that part of me who'd never voted didn't exist. I *cringed* just thinking about what it would mean to examine myself and my life decisions—never mind share that with the world. I felt my mind trying to distract myself or dissociate with work, TV, and social media just to not look at *that*. I felt a lot of shame for allowing myself to keep my head in the sand for such a long time—but when you avoid the truth, it perpetuates the narrative that making mistakes or being a regular human being who is always growing and learning isn't acceptable.

> "One of the great psychological crises of our time is that we live in a culture that demands authenticity and vulnerability, yet denies and punishes the shadow."
>
> NEIL STRAUSS

As a Content Creator, you will always have parts of you that you'll feel called to share more of that may feel easier to just . . . hide. But when you choose *not* to hide, you move closer to taking full ownership of the parts of yourself you previously felt were shameful. Consider the incredible Creators who have shared images of themselves in swimsuits with their tummy rolls, stretch marks, and makeup-free faces. That may have been easy for some, but for many, it absolutely required a lot of inner work, therapy, community support, and finally releasing the narrative that they are not defined by what their bodies look like *before* they could even consider posting these pictures unapologetically.

Another important element of the shadow is that there can be a "shadow side" or "shadow expression" to everything. Let's look at marketers, for example. When marketers are at their best, they're creating visibility and awareness for brands through different strategies, language, images, videos, and audio to attract and sell to the correct customers. There's nothing inherently wrong or immoral about this—especially when those customers are satisfied with their purchases. The positively regarded side of marketing is that the right people can find and purchase the products they want.

However, the dark side of marketing includes manipulation through abusive and hyperbolic language. Marketers have lied and stretched the truth for years and years to make money. Have you ever felt like you didn't want to market to your audience to not be sleazy, pushy, or seen as one of "those" people? Great—you were aware that there's a dark side to marketing you didn't want to be a part of but realize that, without awareness, you could have been.

This kind of fear or hesitation of being (or being seen as) a certain way—whether sexual, powerful, vulnerable, influential, too much, or otherwise—is a signal, directing us to what lives in our shadow. Being a sexual person could be seen as shadowy, dark, unconscious, or immoral—but when integrated and claimed in a healthy way, it's liberating, powerful, pleasurable, and connective. Powerful people can have a lot of hate thrown at them, especially if they aren't using their power for good—like using shady or unethical marketing tactics or evading social responsibility during important social movements. However, they could also use that power to share their voice or resources and effect meaningful change in the world. The human experience will *always* have a shadow expression to it—and the only way to truly feel confident, whole, and in more acceptance of yourself is to face whatever lives within those spaces, even if you have to go on a vulnerable, introspective journey.

WHAT LIVES IN YOUR SOCIAL MEDIA SHADOW?

What you consciously or unconsciously choose to keep offline is your *social media shadow*, which can include:

- Personal opinions
- Emotional expression or fluctuations
- Mental- or physical-health struggles
- Personal stories or experiences that feel vulnerable
- Perceived failures or mistakes
- Your messier, less put-together physical appearance
- Life changes around which you hold shame, judgment, or fear
- Anything else that feels genuinely vulnerable to you

There are many reasons we hide parts of ourselves from social media. Let's face it: it can be an emotionally dangerous, deregulating, and triggering place within which to merely exist, let alone share the more tender, vulnerable parts of yourself. We all have defense mechanisms built to keep us safe from that pain in real life, never mind in the "Wild Wild Web" full of strangers, trolls, and people who will never fully understand us.

"These treasures try desperately to emerge, to come to our attention, but we are conditioned to push them back down. Like giant beach balls being held underwater, these aspects pop back up to the surface whenever we take the pressure off. By choosing not to allow parts of ourselves to exist, we are forced to expend huge amounts of psychic energy to keep them beneath the surface."

DEBORAH FORD, *THE DARK SIDE OF THE LIGHT CHASERS*

A famous piece of writing from Camille Rainville (which went viral in a video where actress-turned-activist Cynthia Nixon read it) represents what it feels like to be judged simply for existing as a normal human being:

> Be a lady they said. Don't talk too loud. Don't talk too much. Don't take up space. Don't sit like that. Don't stand like that. Don't be intimidating. Why are you so miserable? Don't be a bitch. Don't be so bossy. Don't be assertive. Don't overact. Don't be so emotional. Don't cry. Don't yell. Don't swear. Be passive. Be obedient. Endure the pain. Be pleasing. Don't complain.[8]

Even if you don't identify as a woman, you can likely relate to the confusion of being told contradictory messages about how the world expects you to be. As young children, we learned the expectations placed on us through our experiences. If we cried, threw a temper tantrum, or got bullied, picked on, punished, or otherwise, we learned that certain aspects or expressions of ourselves were unacceptable. Maybe you got bullied as a child and learned that you needed to be quiet in a corner to protect yourself. Or perhaps you responded with rage and vengeance, finding that hurting those bullies back made bearing your own pain easier. Those childhood experiences contributed to the formation of your social strategy, which correlates to how you'll handle criticism as an adult in the online realm, be it from dedicated trolls, disputatious colleagues, or disgruntled customers.

Will you marshal your resources and wage a counterassault against those who dare threaten you or impugn your honor? Perhaps shift into passivity, obsequiously apologizing to end the conflict? Or will you go dark for a month, disappearing from the internet in fear?

I want you to ask yourself right now:

- What have I intentionally or unintentionally hidden from social media to protect myself?
- What were my fears, concerns, or worries about sharing?
- What does it feel like for me to not share this?

In 2019, one of my business coaching clients, Heather, went through a challenging time in her life that prompted her to take a social media break and recenter herself. During her break from constant content consumption and creation, Heather realized how much pressure she was putting on herself to show up a certain way and how it was depleting her energy. Upon her return to social media, she decided to share her experience and process with her audience—rather than pretend it didn't happen. Sharing allowed her to release any shame she may have had about taking a break and reconnected to what was true: needing a break, taking a pause, or struggling doesn't make you weak—it's just a part of life. To her surprise, the truly vulnerable share provided her a beautiful reference point that sharing something difficult could actually be well received.

Years before we met, my now-husband John (also an author and Content Creator) shared his experience with depression and suicidal ideation in a seven-thousand-word essay posted to his site and shared across his social accounts. At that point, laying bare his mental-health struggles terrified him. In the years since, he's written that publishing the essay allowed him to feel more and more comfortable allowing people to know when he's struggling. Certain bells cannot be un-rung, and once the world knew about his mental-health issues, he stopped trying to manage other people's experiences of him. Whereas once John would try to work when he felt incapable while spending energy hiding his depression, he is now very open about what he struggles with. He let the world know he was suffering, and the world did not judge him or leave him—and through this, he was able to find acceptance from others and himself.

Just like Heather and John, you'll likely need to go through a process of being vulnerable, open, and honest with *yourself* before you take your story public. This may require you to confront the judgments you've placed on yourself for buying into the belief that these parts of you are not okay. Now, those judgments can run deep—especially if they have roots in any kind of trauma. But the key to this process is remembering that more fully accepting yourself is a gradual practice of giving yourself love, acceptance, and tenderness in the areas where you used to be insensitive or harsh.

Take a moment right now to practice thinking about a part of yourself you judge harshly. Picture it in your mind—what does it look like? How do you speak to it? When you've connected to it, slowly start shifting those automatic thoughts to some intentional, different ones and see how it feels. Then, place your hand on your heart and say, "I love you. I'm sorry. I forgive you. Thank you." This is a simple yet impactful statement—coming from the Hawaiian healing practice of ho'oponopono. When you can forgive yourself for judging yourself, it will become far easier to bring that part of you into the online space to share with others.

Sharing your social media shadow is a courageous practice of witnessing, taking responsibility for, and claiming the parts of yourself you thought were unacceptable—too much, too little, not quite right, too wrong, too inconsiderate, too *whatever*. You can't always trust every stranger to hold you in compassion, but when you press "Post" on that one piece of content and stand in your newly integrated truth, it will change your life.

YOU DON'T OWE ANYONE YOUR VULNERABILITY

The content you choose to create is entirely up to you: what you share, when you share, and how vulnerable you decide to be. If you're a YouTube vlogger going through a breakup from a relationship that was public, it may feel like you owe your followers an explanation. In fact, you may even want to share your side of the story. But it is always your choice to share the level of vulnerability and openness that feels right for you. Any type of new relationship, relationship breakdown, health problem, family issue, political debate, or work struggle will inevitably invite commentary. As we've learned so far in this book, not all the commentary directed toward you will come from a loving place. In fact, most people's comments will come from their own projected, internal experience of their life and the world—and how whatever you shared does or doesn't fit into their worldview. Maybe you just had a child and don't want to cross the boundaries of your infant before they are available to consent, so you don't post pictures of your newborn. Maybe other people in your space show more of their bodies and get a lot of attention, and you used to do that, but you don't desire to do that anymore. Bottom line: even if you've shared vulnerable, intimate moments with your audience before, you can revoke privileges to your vulnerability at *any* given point in time—period.

Oftentimes, however, sharing a vulnerable story publicly can become a beautiful healing opportunity. For me, writing or sharing has always been a truly empowering way to reclaim my pain, eradicate shame, and practice self-acceptance. I've frequently opted to keep many of those very personal, contextual, nuanced moments to myself, using my discernment to know when something is just for me or something to share and express with the world.

Another challenge you'll need to navigate is what to do when you're feeling emotional, mentally drained, or energetically low—when you want to show up authentically but worry about sharing while you're in a negative place. Moreover, you'll have to navigate energy management; if you normally maintain a certain cadence with your Instagram stories or posting content, a few weeks in the doldrums can hinder productivity—and then you'll feel guilty about not producing. You'll feel bad about feeling bad. Many of the clients in my business coaching practice have shared their struggles with feeling like they need to show up online but not having the energy to create content. Unless you can compartmentalize extremely well, it can be difficult to put on a happy face for your audience.

According to *Psychology Today*, "Compartmentalization is a defense mechanism in which people mentally separate conflicting thoughts, emotions, or experiences to avoid the discomfort of contradiction." Compartmentalization can be a healthy coping tool to "put emotions in a box" until they are ready to be processed, allowing for a temporary respite from emotional overload.[9]

Choosing what vulnerable things you might share can feel internally conflicting for Creators, as it's become a well-known engagement and marketing tool to "share a vulnerable story." Because, honestly, it does work. What many Creators find after sharing a new part of themselves is that their core audience connects even more deeply with them. I've had hundreds of clients go through a transitional phase or share an experience that was emotionally difficult and end up receiving amazing feedback from their audiences. Oftentimes, those posts get extremely high levels of engagement from community members who relate and feel seen in the emotion of the story—creating a potential anchor that sharing vulnerably will get you praise and love, even if it doesn't feel completely aligned on the inside.

In October of 2022, I shared a three-part story series highlighting an experience I found particularly vulnerable to share—which was that I'd had the lowest revenue year in business yet and was struggling financially and having bouts of depression and anxiety as a result. As a business coach who people generally saw always coaching and guiding other people on how to make money, sharing my experience shattered this vision people may have had of me as someone who always had my shit together when it came to money and getting business. As scary as it was to share that, I knew how important it was to normalize fluctuations in revenue, confusion and frustration as a business owner, and prioritizing other areas of life before business. It ended up being the first time in months that I had an overflow of comments and messages from my community telling me how they resonated with my story and how just reading it helped unlock things for them—specifically, feeling less alone in their own struggles and releasing shame around their relationship with money.

Storytelling is the way humans connect with each other, after all. When stories are shared, we're able to empathize emotionally with the person sharing their story, even if we haven't gone through the same experience. I've shared so many aspects of my life online—from silly dance moves, to crying and emotional moments, to my polyamorous relationship—all in front of hundreds of thousands of humans. But if I've learned anything from sharing my journey vulnerably, it's that I usually do not share until I've reconciled most of the internal doubts, fear-based narratives, and shame within myself before I share with the world. A great marker of when it's a good time to share a story is how prepared you feel to handle comments and questions that may feel like personal attacks and judgments you've probably already felt inside of your own mind and body. Remember: this journey is all about finding what feels authentic and self-honoring to you as a Content Creator, and that includes not needing to take on more emotional labor than is really necessary.

Here are some questions to ask yourself when discerning what to share:

- If I share this today, am I emotionally prepared to handle the potential comments, opinions, and judgments from people who—although I'm sharing about a tender part of my heart and self—will never truly know me?
- If I share, where am I coming from? What is my intention? What's my desired outcome? Is now the best time for me to share this, or will writing about my situation without posting be just as powerful for me?
- What are the implications of my share? Who does it affect? Am I comfortable with those implications and prepared to deal with them?

THE SOCIAL MEDIA PERSONA

While you ponder facing your shadows and bringing out more of those hidden elements of yourself, we can't forget to talk about your social media *persona:* the "you" your audience sees. Your social media handle. Your name in air quotes. The "you" who pops up in your followers' minds when they think about you—created by what you've chosen to share online. If the shadow internally hides itself so as to evade being found, the persona outwardly projects itself to be seen and witnessed.

Psychotherapist Amy Morin shares that "Once you draw a conclusion about yourself, you're likely to do two things; look for evidence that reinforces your belief and discount anything that runs contrary to your belief."[10] This is why social media is, in fact, a highlight reel that doesn't show anything bad or negative! We're *designed* to share what we believe are the best parts of ourselves that help us receive the most amount of love and acceptance and that allow us to feel comfortable in front of others. This is the version of ourselves that our audiences follow and have a relationship with. Of course, this version is not the full you—it's just the "you" that you've chosen to offer to the public.

Speaking from a childhood-development level, if you were praised, provided love, or rewarded for your looks, accomplishments, ability to not bother anyone, or any other perceived "positive" quality, you learned to keep sharing that with the world. As you grew up, those behaviors anchored in as ingrained patterns, leading to continuous reward, praise, and love. When we get online, we're projecting our internal experience onto the external playground of social media—including all of those behavioral patterns that help us feel accepted, welcomed, loved, praised, and supported. This is how your online persona forms—and why it can feel like you have to continue "dressing up" as that persona sometimes long after you've evolved past it.

Your subconscious patterns from childhood won't be the only reason you may struggle to shift your online persona and share more parts of yourself. For so many Creators, it's difficult to anticipate the likelihood of losing followers or watching your engagement decrease because of how linked those metrics can be to either your livelihood, sense of identity, or both. If your engagement or follower count decreases after you post something genuine and authentic to you and your life path, it may feel like who you are isn't okay or enough.

I once spoke with a travel influencer who had shared her life adventures and world travels for five years and was scared about what it meant for her brand to settle down and stop traveling for a while. On a brand-development level, I discuss exactly how to navigate a change like that in chapter eleven, "Pivoting Powerfully." But on a personal, identity, and self-awareness level, the key to processing this experience emotionally is to start by setting the intention to experience the freedom to be authentic.

By the time a personal story, perspective, or idea makes it to your socials, it'll already have passed many mental and emotional "acceptability" tests you send your potential content through to ensure its acceptability. Some thoughts or fears you may find are swirling around in your mind before you post could sound like:

- Is this good enough?
- What will people think of this?
- Is this part of me allowed here?
- Will I be judged, shamed, or cast out for sharing about this?

Where do you feel stuck in your brand and content direction—perhaps even disengaged, unmotivated, and apathetic toward your social media content? This may be a sign that you're disconnected from your authentic voice or expression as a Content Creator. Perhaps you want to break out of the persona character you've been playing and do something a bit different, but don't feel like you know how—or that it's even okay.

So far in this book, you've learned a lot about how to face the kinds of fears that arise when it comes to shifting your online presence. This next section is about how to do shadow work and will teach you how to look at the most challenging parts of yourself so that you can take ownership of and integrate them.

HOW TO DO SHADOW WORK

When we don't address or confront the shadow, it ends up unconsciously seeping through the cracks of our psyche into thoughts, emotions, and actions as a projection of the internal world in the external, material reality. This is called *shadow repression*.

In late 2019, I was invited to a retreat in Costa Rica to participate in a ceremony with the plant medicine ayahuasca. Used by indigenous peoples for around a thousand years, ayahuasca is served as a tea brewed from two plants to create a psychedelic experience for the purposes of uncovering memories and working through emotional blocks. During the ceremony, I experienced what it felt like to confront my own shadows in a place I lovingly titled "the swamp where repressed emotions go to fester." Two hours into this psychedelic plant-medicine ceremony in the jungle, I experienced myself (in my mind's eye) to be in a mucky, sticky, dark swamp that felt gross. During my process of trying to make sense of this symbolism, I realized that this represented the place where I pushed down emotions, and they had started to fester internally—causing chaos in real life. This experience also reminded me of the challenges of shadow work—it may not feel easy to see the parts of yourself you haven't liked or accepted, maybe for your whole life.

Shadow work is a *lifelong* practice of looking at the rejected, criticized, disowned, shamed, or not-"okay" aspects of ourselves through a lens of curiosity, love, and acceptance. In this process of bringing what's in the shadow into the light, we can actually acknowledge more of who we are, clear out the energies of shame and "wrongness," and become more whole. Integrating parts of yourself—whether it's your inner bitch, your inner emotional crier, your inner judgmental asshole, or your inner powerful online educator—with shadow work can create a sense of feeling more whole and at peace internally. This is *shadow integration.*

Integration is about accepting the whole self by working to accept the various parts that have been deemed unacceptable. For example, you embrace being both selfish and selfless, realizing not only that you need both of them but also that neither one of them is actually bad. In fact, any characteristic can have a shadow expression to it. For example, selfishness can look like being inconsiderate to others, which someone could view as immoral. But on the flip side, selflessness—which is typically viewed as moral—can manifest as martyrdom or abandonment of your own needs to serve other people, which is not good, either. Funnily enough, the way you heal and integrate martyrdom is through demonstrating healthy selfishness—including setting and enforcing boundaries, choosing and prioritizing yourself first, and saying no to things that will energetically drain you. So is selfishness truly "wrong," or can it simply be a version of relating to yourself that can sometimes look like being inconsiderate of others and an unintegrated sense of selflessness? Rather than viewing parts of yourself as bad or wrong, shadow work calls for us to view all parts of ourselves as important, and the rejection and exile of any of them is not actually the path to becoming a good person.

followed

The shadow's nature craves to be seen, heard, and integrated. Think about it like this: "you" are both the observer of what you do and the one who does it all. Often, the subconscious patterns and the inner witness are out of sync and disconnected—which can make you feel like you are not truly in the driver's seat of your own life. When you practice becoming the witness of your thoughts, feelings, behaviors, and shadows, you can experience more harmony internally, all of your parts effectively communicating and collaborating with each other. You are the author of your own book, and your parts (like your shadow and persona), are simply the characters. I personally like to think of the parts inside of me forming my inner council. The more an observer can build a healthy relationship with and nurture their shadow, the smaller the shadow gets.

When you're looking to feel more confident and authentic as a Content Creator, doing shadow work can help being on social media feel lighter and more relaxed. The more you accept yourself and the statements you actually want to make online, the more real, raw, polarizing, and authentic your content will be.

Here are some symptoms of an unintegrated social media shadow:

- Feeling defensive when criticized
- Reactively blocking or arguing with everyone who upsets you
- Avoiding posting polarizing content
- Avoiding sharing your story or experience, hiding, and feeling like an imposter
- Curating your feed perfectly
- Only showing up when you feel amazing

Here are some signs of an integrated social media shadow:

- Ability to hold a conversation and integrate the lessons of criticisms
- Openness to opinions and perspectives other than your own
- Audience feels safe to share the vulnerable parts of themselves with you

- Consistently posting polarizing, unique-to-you content with confidence
- Consistently sharing your story and experience
- Posting content and images that feel authentic to you
- Showing up when you feel all emotions, holding yourself with compassion, and leading with authentic vulnerability
- People seeing you for who you truly are; feeling free and liberated regardless of who follows you or unfollows you

HOW TO BEGIN IDENTIFYING YOUR SHADOWS

In the process of leaning into my own shadow work, I always giggle when I notice my ego making its best attempt to have me avoid looking at it. The most recent example has been in my relationship, where my husband John gave me some feedback about how I can show up for him better than I have been. For a few days, I got defensive about it. All I could talk about was all the evidence in my relationship where I have been an *amazing* partner rather than simply listening to his truth and experience. I avoided confronting my shadow: the part of me that is selfish and self-centered. The avoidance of looking at that comes from my rejection and shame around my own selfishness and the way my ego clung onto the "nice, helpful person" projection of who I believe myself to be. But after a lot of processing, I can now see that my shadow simply needed to be integrated in order for me to really take responsibility and take better actions moving forward.

If you do have the courage to face your shadow, know that it's okay if you notice it coming up again and again. The goal is to continue your practice of not shaming it and to instead see it as an unintegrated part that wants to be seen and met—and to keep practicing. For some aspects of your shadow, however, you may want to minimize what you find or only go partway and then decide you've done enough on that front. For example: I'm very aware that I have a huge fear of roller coasters, adrenaline, and anything involving potential serious physical injury, and I have no intention of doing the work to integrate that side of myself. Maybe one day, but I'm happy to keep that door closed as it's really not affecting my life in any major way.

Shadow work isn't for the fainthearted, so below are some simple suggestions to get you started.

- Accept that you do, in fact, have shadows everywhere—and expect them to tell you where and who they are in emotionally challenging situations in your life. Signs your shadow is at play include:
  - Judging yourself
  - Judging other people
  - Defensiveness
  - Deflecting
  - Centering yourself
  - Justification
  - Avoidance
  - Anxiety
- Ground yourself in compassionate self-forgiveness. Your shadow isn't bad, and we all have our own shadows, so you may have feelings associated with it that need to be acknowledged, expressed, and worked through. Try the prompt "I forgive myself for judging myself for/as . . ." and hold yourself lovingly. This may be difficult, and that's okay, too.
- You may be able to process and navigate some parts of your shadow on your own, but many of them will have memories or trauma attached to them, in which case it's important to consider a safe, healing space with the support of a professional therapist or coach.

As you begin identifying and exploring your shadows, remember: these parts of you simply want to be seen, witnessed, and integrated into your perception of self. When you do this, you'll end up feeling more whole. Consider yourself as the loving, nurturing parent to these parts of you. The better relationship you can build with them, determining what they want and need to feel safe and loved, the easier it will be to integrate them.

Identify Your Social Media Shadows Exercise

If you want more clarity on your own social media shadow so you can start working on your growth in this area, head to followedbook.io to fill out the journal prompts for this exercise so you can identify your social media shadows.

Identify a struggle you've been having in relation to social media recently. Maybe you feel like you'll never grow your audience or you feel icky taking pictures of yourself. Maybe you've shared vulnerably, and people have criticized you for it. Write down: What is upsetting about the other person, yourself, or the situation?

Identify, express, and explore the feelings present from this experience. What are your feelings about this experience? Give yourself permission to explore and express your feelings honestly. If your feelings had a voice, what would each one say?

What (or who) does this situation (or person) remind me of from my past?

What am I avoiding looking at or feeling? What are you afraid of? What's the worst-case scenario?

Write out the best-case scenario for this situation: a vision that feels inspiring. And then ask these questions:

- What parts of me do I anticipate will mess this all up?
- What voices inside of me say I can't or shouldn't do this?

You'll know when you're in resistance because you'll find yourself coming up with reasons why a scenario can't or shouldn't happen, why it's impossible, or why it's a struggle for you. These are the voices of your unconscious parts, or your shadow.

What benefit do I receive from engaging in this dynamic in the way I am? In other words: some part of you receives some sort of benefit from playing into the dynamic. What could that benefit be? Some examples include: getting to stay comfortable, not having to have a difficult conversation, and not needing to face the consequences of making change.

What is this situation or person mirroring back to me about my relationship with myself? What part of you is being mirrored back to you by this person or situation? What part of yourself do you meet in the dynamic with this person?

Offer yourself compassionate self-forgiveness. Here are some healing words you can say to yourself, taken from the University of Santa Monica's spiritual-psychology program. I invite you to forgive yourself for buying into any limiting beliefs, misinterpretations of reality, or misidentifications of yourself. Complete this sentence as many times as needed:

"I forgive myself for buying into the misbelief/judgment that [insert a negative belief or judgment you've adopted about yourself], and the truth is [insert an upgraded belief you want to adopt here instead]."

Here's an example: "I forgive myself for buying into the misbelief that I am not worthy of love, that I'm not enough, that I'm a bad person, that I'm not loveable, etc., and the truth is that I was doing the best I could with what I had at the time, and I am still worthy of love."

When working with your own social media shadow, use this as a reminder that it's not about what content you create or what mood you're in on any given day. It's your relationship to yourself that influences who shows up in your space. You don't need to be happy all the time to attract the audience members who will connect with you the most. You simply have to accept yourself as you are and allow yourself to be in the process.

Critics, Haters, Trolls—Oh My!

When dealing with critics, haters, or trolls, how often have you heard this trite advice:

"You can be the juiciest peach in the patch, and someone just won't like peaches."

Or:

"They're probably just some idiot living in their mom's basement."

This type of consolation might be well intentioned—but it doesn't really help Content Creators navigate the intensity of incendiary conflict. Every Creator has some level of resistance to, hesitation on, and fear of being judged online! And the fear isn't unsubstantiated: as you yourself have likely witnessed rude comments about someone's appearance, comment section battles, or even full-fledged cancellation campaigns. Braving [illegible] yourself, your emotional state, your mental health, and your reputation [illegible]. With greater visibility come more opportunities to be misunderstood, and more chances for your work to trigger someone.

eight

Critics, Haters, Trolls—*Oh My!*

When dealing with critics, haters, or trolls, how often have you heard this trite advice?

"You can be the juiciest peach in the patch, and someone just won't like peaches!"

Or:

"They're probably just some idiot living in their mom's basement!"

This type of consolation might be well intentioned—but it doesn't *really* help Content Creators navigate the intensity of internet conflict. Every Creator has some level of resistance to, hesitation to, and fear of being judged online. And it's not unsubstantiated, as you yourself have likely witnessed rude comments about someone's appearance, comments-section battles, or even full-fledged cancellation campaigns. Fearing for yourself, your emotional state, your mental health, and your reputation makes sense. With greater visibility come more opportunities to be misunderstood and more chances for your existence to trigger someone else.

For a very long time on the internet, the standard of behavior was that Content Creators, influencers, and educators would "stay in their lane." But after 2020 unfolded with the pandemic and Black Lives Matter movement, the entire culture shifted to demanding transparency from influencers, Creators, brands, and companies about their political views, personal values, and belief systems so we could vote with our dollars and attention. All of a sudden, no one could hide.

As content consumers, we've become increasingly picky with who we follow and the ways in which we allow those people—or their content—to influence us. And rightly so. Consumers haven't just become more discerning, they've become more critical. Which means Content Creators are facing far more criticism than ever before. Dealing with that criticism is a job unto itself, requiring patience, fortitude, and discernment.

That discernment is critical, because the fact is, some of what's hurled at you isn't simply unfounded insult. Some criticism is, in fact, valuable feedback. The tools in this chapter show you how to face the judgment of others in a way that's nuanced and practical. You'll see why the old advice "ignoring the haters" or the idea that you can simply stop caring about what others think isn't just unrealistic but damaging. We'll examine the underlying power dynamics between Creators and consumers and how that dynamic plays a part in highly personal experiences to broader concepts like cancel culture. You'll learn strategies for self-regulation and some insights on what to do if or when you find yourself being called out.

ANYONE CAN SAY ANYTHING: THE MISUSE OF POWER

The valid reason people get criticized online is primarily that people can misuse their power. Before we get into the differences between haters, trolls, and critics, let's acknowledge that influencers, educators, content creators, or people who seek to build an audience are seeking to put themselves in a place of either inherent or inherited power.

We're conditioned to impart trust to anyone who speaks to us in a one-to-many format; this is endemic to our cultural experience. Beginning with our teachers, anyone "at the front of the room" has a level of authority we're taught to give credence to; they stand as we sit, disseminating information we're told is truth. This continues throughout our life. For most of the history of media, a person with a platform had some level of credibility, usually in the form of formalized expertise—talking heads or radio hosts were usually journalists or pundits. That began to shift with celebrity culture when we started to care not only about what movie stars and musicians did in their spare time but what they thought about pressing issues.

Social media created a new kind of public figure—and as celebrity culture gave rise to influencer culture, the line between expert and entertainer blurred and blurred. Now, in a world in which we get our news from Twitter and YouTubers who rose to prominence as practical jokers become political commentators, it's clear that our societal conditioning leads us to conflate familiarity with authority.

Simply said, popularity is a kind of power—and like all power, it can be abused. This is true for every Content Creator, even those in the most benign industries or with relatively small audiences. The truth is, you can unconsciously take advantage of and exploit that. Or you can make the choice to become aware of it and actively work to avoid it. Creators are taught to become "marketable" by saying things people want to hear, or presenting a version of themselves that will help them capitalize and gain more money, power, and respect. How does doing that work to your benefit, but more importantly—create potential harm?

We must remember that the nature of what we do as Content Creators requires—as part of the recipe for success—*accumulation*. We need to garner attention. Influence requires interest; we need to keep eyeballs on us. We need people to trust us so they keep coming back. If we're not careful, we can fall out of integrity to make that happen. We can misuse that trust.

If we do—and, often, even if we don't—there's a whole internet's worth of sharp-eyed and sharp-clawed people ready to let us (and the rest of the world) know about it. As we move into the rest of the chapter and examine the types of people who may engage with us in ways we find difficult, keep in mind that while, yes, some people will hate on and even harass you no matter what you do, others are there to reflect back the ways you can be better. That's the difference between a hater and a critic. And a troll? Well, that's another creature altogether.

THE THREE OPPOSITIONAL AVATARS: TROLLS, HATERS, AND CRITICS

We can never truly know the full experience of the person we're interacting with on the other side of the screen. One small comment may lead us to believe something about someone's entire character, and that's not helpful on either end of a conversation. But at the very least, start by getting curious about what level of dialogue is possible with this person. Let's talk about the three oppositional avatars: *trolls*, *haters*, and *critics*.

1. **Trolls:** These commenters are often petty, ridiculous, outlandish, unreasonable, and/or disrespectful. They make comments like "You're a dumb bitch" from an anonymous account. These people are *agents of chaos*—finding ways to say whatever the hell they want without considering consequence. The messages tend to be either one-hit wonders or extremely short and repetitive. There's no productive discussion to be had with a troll. As much as they're still a person on the other end of the conversation, there's no real reason to engage with them. Here's an example from the Mean Tweets segment on *Jimmy Kimmel Live*: "I can't stand this new Ed Sheeran.

Like why TF are you happy on your records? You're a f****n ginger for ******'s sake. Be sad."

2. **Haters:** To a hater, you often represent something they believe is wrong, immoral, shameful, or harmful to other people in the world. Maybe how you're showing up directly reminds them of their mother who tried to control their life. Perhaps you look like a person who bullied them in high school. Maybe you have a strong oppositional opinion, and they are committed to tearing you down to lift themselves up. You and this person will not typically find a mutual understanding because you're arguing against each other's deeply rooted, identity-based beliefs. Haters are typically *committed to misunderstanding you.* Oftentimes, haters will project a character, avatar, or identity onto you that doesn't line up with your true self. To a hater, anything you do and say will be another reason to continue disliking you. It's possible to turn a hater into a follower, but you may need to navigate through more heavy conflict and heightened emotions to get there.
3. **Critics:** Critics may or may not articulate their opinions or beliefs in the most considerate way, but the difference between a hater and a critic is that critics are more open to hearing you while also wanting to be heard. Critics will share their opinion, call out gaps in your thinking, hold you accountable to added context, or want you to consider another perspective. Think of this person as your *personalized devil's advocate.* One way or another, they're there to mirror you and your limitations back to you and hold you accountable. They may not necessarily come off as brash, rude, or committed to misunderstanding you—but will rather embody the "call out to call forward" energy. Think of the critic as a person providing feedback and information about how they perceive you. It doesn't always mean their perception is accurate, but it's good information to have that, if considered, could impact the way you continue to show up.

Social media content creation cannot be controlled by an external source without it turning into censorship. We must be free to say what we want, even if that means that some people will make inappropriate comments or engage in behavior we deem bad. Of course, the internet is filled with darkness and problematic behavior—but we cannot force people to value integrity and personal responsibility through shaming, cancellation, and censorship. What we *can* do is encourage Content Creators to be intentional about what they post and ask them to pay attention to:

- The information they share, spread, advocate for, or speak about
- The potential impact that information may have on consumers and audience members
- The unconscious patterns we may be playing out through our content to get some sort of need met (projection, people pleasing, perfectionism, self-sabotage, fear of judgment, etc.)

Other People's Opinions of You Have (*Mostly*) Nothing to Do with You

Think of the dynamic between you and your audience as a relationship. They follow you, connect with you, learn from you, and are impacted by your presence online in one way or another. Although these are primarily parasocial relationships, those in your audience still affect you and your life, and you impact and affect their lives. It's still a relationship.

According to www.findapsychologist.org, parasocial relationships "are one-sided relationships, where one person extends emotional energy, interest and time, and the other party, the persona [or celebrity, politician, influencer, or Content Creator], is completely unaware of the other's existence . . . Studies show parasocial relationships are voluntary, provide companionship, and are influenced by social attraction. Furthermore, viewers experience a connection with the media user and express feelings of affection, gratitude, longing, encouragement, and loyalty towards them."[11]

In all relationships, we can only view the other person through our individual lens of perception. This lens is built on our lived experiences and judgment of the world. Think of your mind as the projector of a movie and the world as what you see on the "screen." This is how two people can look at the same exact situation and have entirely different judgments and opinions.

Now think about yourself and your audience. Every single person following you is projecting their own movie in their minds onto you, seeing what you post through their lens of perception. Some may find your video about limiting beliefs and changing your mindset inspiring, and others may view it as cringey, cheesy, and performative. As much as it may feel like we know a Creator based on what they post, we can only ever know so much—and will never understand the full context of their personality or character. Sometimes the feedback or judgments other people have of us hold some level of truth, and sometimes—it can be helpful to receive that feedback. But as a general rule, the opinion of someone who follows you online can only ever be so accurate and often says more about their worldview than it does about the truth of who you are.

When I received my first mean online comments, they rocked my world. I was so used to receiving extremely positive and uplifting comments from my followers. With so much external validation coming at me on a regular basis, I believed all the praise. It wasn't until I started gaining more visibility that the more crude, hateful, and judgmental comments came in. People told me I came across as inauthentic and dumb, like I didn't know what I was talking about. Some of them emphasized how much they hated my voice. Simply put, they made it clear: I was *not* for them. That experience taught me that regardless of what I did or how much I tried to be perfect or likable, there would always be some people in the world who just wouldn't understand me—and that's okay.

This is where I learned to practice not letting the negative *or* the positive comments affect my view of myself. Giving the positive comments *too* much power over me was just as detrimental as letting the negative comments get to me. If we allow our self-image to be very puffed up when people give us positive validation, it'll also mean we'll become more vulnerable to feeling poorly or becoming negatively affected when people say unkind or hurtful things to us. In that state, you'd be living from your ego—rather than being connected to your core, authentic self.

Block, Delete, Ignore, or Respond?

Audience members who criticize Creators often use the argument "you chose to put yourself in the spotlight—being criticized comes with the territory" to justify their behavior when offering feedback. This type of statement borders along the same line as "You chose to wear that short skirt; anything that happens is on you," or "I'm extremely angry at you, so I have the right to be an asshole right now."

Regardless of how emotional you are, we all have the choice to be responsible for how we show up or react in those emotions. Having a public platform does not automatically mean you chose to be okay with rude, hateful, or harmful dialogue—you still get to set boundaries and teach people how you are and aren't available to be treated. Your social media platform is still your own little home on the internet, and everyone who finds you actively chooses to be there. You are not forcing anyone to follow you or be in your space, and in that vein, you should not be forced to engage with anyone who isn't treating you or your space with respect. Again—we are in some form of a relationship with our audience members, so we may genuinely want to show up for them, listen to them, respond to their messages, and be in connection with them. But for the sake of the sanity and mental health of both creators and consumers, it's important to clarify what we can expect from one another in the context of these kind of relationships.

All relationships require boundaries—which include the behaviors we do not tolerate, are not available for, and will not engage in. We teach our audience members how to treat us, and they are within their rights to set boundaries with us if they feel hurt as well. Because we don't know most of our audience members intimately, we have to keep our expectations in check. It's important for both parties to recognize the relationship for what it is and not project unfair or unrealistic expectations onto one another. No one is obliged to follow us, agree with us, or validate us. We are not obliged to agree with, follow, or validate other people. We do not need to explain every action we take or don't take online, nor do we need to tolerate it when others place expectations upon us.

This is where online boundaries come in. The boundaries you set and the way you decide to maintain your inner peace on your platform are entirely up to you. Feel free to go back to chapter five if you want to look more broadly at your boundaries when it comes to social media.

To a *troll* or a person blatantly disrespecting you—feel free to *block*, *delete*, or *ignore*. I personally block people who make obviously rude comments that either affect me or my audience members negatively, no reflection needed. You may have been told that blocking or deleting comments is silencing people's voices or that it looks like you're hiding something. I've been told this many times—but the important point to remember is this: your social platform is like your home. You aren't obligated to explain your boundaries to people who seem committed to misunderstanding you. Maybe you are, in fact, hiding a part of your life that you don't want to explain to the entire internet, or maybe you prefer to keep certain aspects private, or maybe you don't want false opinions about you or a situation sitting in your comments section. Because you're not obliged to explain that situation, this means you are well within your rights to remove comments or messages that may open up doors that you want to stay closed.

Responding to a *hater* is typically where the biggest disagreements, longest comment threads, and most frustration occur. Conversations with haters are usually layered, including but not limited to:

- Opposing worldviews
- Differences in opinion
- Heightened emotions (and an inability to regulate them during the conflict)
- Blame, judgment, and criticism of character
- Defensiveness

A fairly common example is arguing about politics. If you strongly believe abortion is murder, you'll judge people who stand up against abortion bans for not valuing the life of a child. If you're against abortion bans and stand up for human rights and bodily autonomy, you'll judge and argue with people who are pro-life.

Chances are, you and this person will never find mutual ground and understanding because you're arguing against each other's deeply rooted, identity-based beliefs. Be cautious with your responses. Be aware that they may not see you as a real person with feelings but as more of an avatar of a type of person they don't like or agree with. Because you have a platform and a voice, people who disagree with you are more likely to judge you harshly, as your platform is a place for you to share and spread your beliefs with the world—and to them, that may feel wrong. Here are a few ways you can respond to haters:

- You can engage with them and learn from one another.
- You can ignore them and not let their comments affect your peace.
- You can block them if a comment, response, or statement crosses any of your boundaries.

Responding to a *critic* is different. Some comments or messages may feel like an attack on your character, but they may simply be a callout for you to look at or consider a different perspective you may not have considered. As much as other people cannot fully see, know, or understand the whole of your character from your social media platforms, it doesn't mean they can't be mirrors for you to see other perspectives or blind spots. Feeling or experiencing discomfort from what someone says does not automatically mean they're crossing a boundary, attacking you, or being rude. Emotional discomfort (outside of intense triggers that may reactivate trauma) is an arrow pointing to unresolved emotional material within your own consciousness.

Let's say that a follower responds to your post about the differences between women and men. While you were trying to make a point about some of the inherent differences between men and women, someone else who lives outside the gender binary may want to point out that you could have used more inclusive language. You may initially feel triggered—*don't they see that what I'm saying is true?* Perhaps your statement is less about the biology of any specific person and more about how men and women are socialized to embody certain conceptions within a culture. You may feel a bit defensive and may want to fight back to explain your point.

This is a great opportunity to take a moment and consider that this person's perspective may actually be valuable. In this instance, two perspectives can be true at the same time. There are inherent differences between men and women, *and* you could adjust your language in the future to be more inclusive to nonbinary and trans folks. It may be a hit to your ego to feel like you did something wrong, but next time, say this: "I didn't think of it that way; thank you for showing me another perspective."

As a Content Creator and privileged cis white woman who grew up in an upper-middle-class family, I was incredibly naive as to how my limited worldview impacted my content and the people who followed me. Through sitting and listening to critics and people wanting to hold me accountable, I've grown more than I could have ever imagined as my following size has grown. Being open to having real conversations with people in my DMs who respond to what I say with a different perspective—even when they sometimes have a judgment or emotional charge attached to them—has changed me for the better.

TAKE A BEAT: REGULATING YOUR EMOTIONAL STATE

When I went through my cancellation experience, I spent three days in a dissociative fugue state as people attacked my character. I found it to be one of the most emotionally deregulating times of my life. My internal threat-protection systems were firing on all cylinders as I found my body undulating through waves of anger, fear, shame, embarrassment, and hypervigilance. If you've ever had even a small internet argument, it's likely you also remember having feelings about it—feelings ranging from annoyance to immobilization, to depression and intense anxiety.

A client of mine once told me how nervous she was to receive any kind of criticism or judgment online due to her traumatic history of being bullied. Many others have shared with me how they wouldn't know if they'd be able to handle going through a public shaming like I did. Having so many eyeballs on you, judging you, and criticizing you and feeling fairly defenseless can be very overwhelming. In fact, it should be taken very seriously, especially for trauma survivors or those with preexisting mental-health diagnoses or challenges.

What you might experience is highly dependent on how your body responds to stress. In stressful circumstances, do you notice yourself shutting down, struggling to speak? Perhaps you've found yourself in rabbit-hole-style arguments with someone in your comment section, fighting back and forth for hours or days. Maybe you've attempted to get people to see and understand your side, placating when it becomes too much.

First and foremost: the intensity of your experience is completely valid. Social media isn't just a silly place of non-reality—it has a very real impact on your lived experience. It's okay to feel, to not be okay, and to need support, as these experiences can be quite dysregulating, especially if you have any mental-health diagnoses or challenges. If you're feeling dysregulated, it'd be beneficial to seek professional support if you become overwhelmed. If you're seeking additional tools to regulate yourself in the moment, head to the accompanying journal at followedbook.io for recommendations. These tools should not be taken as or replace medical advice. Check with your therapist or mental-health counselor before taking any steps that may affect your well-being.

EFFECTIVELY NAVIGATING CONFLICT IN THE ONLINE SPACE

When you're nervous, hesitant, or scared to create content that feels truthful to you but may be received as polarizing, it's helpful to remember that there are steps you can take to put yourself in a better position to have that content be well received without being inauthentic. Let's talk about how to create a foundation of trust between yourself and your audience.

Establish Clear Expectations

There will always be people who will misunderstand you, have unrealistic expectations of you, project onto you, and judge you through the lens of their limited perception. As much as it's impossible to manage everyone's experience of you, you can lead the way by establishing who you are and what people can expect from you up front—and on your own terms. Creating realistic expectations helps everyone (you and your audience) avoid unnecessary conflict that comes from misunderstandings and unclear expectations.

Clear Expectation 1: Share Disclaimers and Your Limitations

The number of horror stories of people following information from someone they mistakenly believed was an expert is higher than ever now. Being transparent with your limitations will minimize a lot of potential harm. Disclaimers are statements that express the limits of legal liability for the content or information shared. I am not a lawyer, nor should this be taken as legal advice—I'm just a longtime Content Creator and business owner who knows it's important not only to protect yourself but also to be up front and transparent with your audience. Being clear about the limits of your training, expertise, and experience on a semi-regular basis helps your audience contextualize your content before they consume it and apply it to their lives. You're protecting them, too.

A major issue with the content- and information-sharing age is how unregulated and easy it is for people to spread misinformation and negatively affect and impact those who follow them. Most people blindly follow, consume, and integrate information without a second thought about where that information may have come from. Those who are actively skeptical and researchers at heart will always check their sources, but this additional step often gets missed and forgotten when people begin to follow someone with influence, as we implicitly correlate influence with expertise and authority. We often assume a person has done their research, knows what they're talking about, and has enough credibility to be trusted and listened to—which is not always true.

Here are examples of disclaimers:

> "I am not a doctor or therapist, and the content on this site should not be taken as a replacement for medical advice. Speak to a trained professional for your medical, mental, emotional, and behavioral health needs before making any decisions."
>
> "These testimonials are individual experiences, and results may vary. These testimonials are not necessarily representative of all users who use our products."
>
> "This is an affiliate link, but I only promote products and services I use and genuinely stand behind. I've vetted this company, and I align with its values. I use this product multiple times per week. I share honest reviews of the product—what I like and don't like—so you can make an informed decision."

Clear Expectation 2: Be Transparent About Your Privilege, Lived Experience, and Accessibility

I've worked with some incredibly intelligent and well-educated clients in my time. People with PhDs, multiple certifications, licenses, years of experience in their craft—and many have *still* found themselves questioning whether what they're doing is wrong because they've received criticism saying they should be doing it differently. Whether you're reading advice about how to work out, choose what to eat, find a career, parent children, or water plants, it's important to first contextualize *who* is saying that information and *what* their experience of life is. If you're a mother of two children under five and you hear "You need to wake up at 5:30 AM every day to do your morning routine" from a Creator twenty years younger than you without any children, that advice is probably not going to feel helpful. That Content Creator may not have as many barriers as you do to making that happen, and it's clear they don't understand your lived experience or have to live your life. As a consumer, move along and follow Creators who *do* get your lived experience. As a Creator, gently let your audience know that what you say is rooted in your personal experience, and don't forget to acknowledge any privilege.

Here are examples of context setting:

> "As a cis white woman with a large platform, I recognize the power I hold sharing content to large groups of people with whom I'll never meet personally, many of whom have largely different lives and upbringings than I do."
>
> "As much as parts of my upbringing were not privileged, I will recognize that parts of it were to help clarify my position, where it comes from, and how you can interpret my content for yourself."
>
> "This is my personal experience, not to be taken as advice for all."
>
> "Take what I say with a grain of salt; compare against your own experiences only."

Clear Expectation 3: Continue Your Education and Acknowledge Your Level of Knowledge on Any Given Topic

What we say online matters. People hear our point of view, and it sticks with them in one way or another. When you're a person sharing information that may impact and affect people's lives, ensure you're continuing your education regularly. Even if you aren't in the personal-development space, if you reshare a post from another account, it could impact people you follow.

Let's say you're a TikTok Creator and decide to make commentary about a recent documentary. It's helpful, if possible, to let people know how much other information you have on the topic to contextualize your comment. It's impossible to expect all Content Creators (including yourself!) to be experts in every single thing they say and share, and you don't have to be. Just practice being truthful, transparent, and a student of life who is learning lessons along the way. As long as you make it a habit to consider how what you're saying may impact others and actively work toward more intentionality, you're on the right track.

Clear Expectation 4: Keep the Absolutist or Extreme Language to a Minimum

We start edging toward the line of potential harm when we use language that makes it seem like what we're saying is 100 percent true 100 percent of the time. Minimizing harm means agreeing to stay away from absolutist language, like using words or phrases such as "always," "never," or "people like this are [insert adjective here]." Just because you believe in an idea doesn't mean it's 100 percent true, fact, or hard-proven science. Just because you and many other people experience events or situations in a particular way doesn't mean every person has that same experience. Saying "carbs are bad" can be extremely harmful to people who genuinely require carbohydrates to have a healthy, functioning body. Claiming "you should always be meditating" can be incredibly harmful advice for people with PTSD or those working through trauma. Sitting in that type of silent space may feel triggering and unsafe for them. Advising your audience to "post three to five times a day" may overwhelm a person who isn't in a space to do that, such as someone with a disability, chronic illness, children, or depression.

Taking these four expectations into consideration of how other people may receive your content, more and more people will feel relaxed coming into your online space. It might not be a complete solution to preventing online conflicts, but it certainly goes a long way!

THE CANCEL-CULTURE CONVERSATION

The more power a Creator gains in the form of followers, the more influence they have over those followers, companies, and other Creators who back them—and the more difficult it becomes to hold them accountable for their words and actions. There are *thousands*, if not *millions*, of instances of celebrities, politicians, and now Content Creators saying whatever they want on their platform without being held accountable for the impact those words and behaviors may have on others. Calling people out is not a new practice—but what *is* new is the *speed* at which information can travel, snowball, and reach the masses. Within callout and cancel culture, Creators and consumers can feel like they're contributing to a cause they care about and gain power back by holding someone accountable for their actions.

The pros of cancel culture are that it:

- Helps those with less social, political, and financial power to hold people with power accountable
- Gives a voice to disenfranchised, marginalized, or less powerful people
- Helps effect changes on a small and large scale
- Raises standards and professional integrity across various industries

The cons of cancel culture are that it:

- Doesn't hold the people who are doing the calling out accountable when they cross a line, like in the case of:
  - Bullying, violence, threats, shaming, harassment, torment, cruelty, or hate
  - Creating unnecessary financial, reputational, or relational damage
  - Unethical exile from communities
  - Treating people as irredeemable or disposable
- Can lead people to performative accountability rather than genuine accountability and actual change
- May lead to people getting pleasure and enjoyment out of taking someone down
- Can portray the person being called out as automatically "guilty" without giving them a fair chance to be seen in light of all views, opinions, and facts

The challenge with the way we, as a collective, tend to handle *holding others accountable* is how quickly we may justify dehumanizing the person being called out. In a personal-development sense: just because someone makes us feel angry doesn't mean they are responsible for our anger—nor is it a justifiable excuse for poor behavior. Regardless of how we feel, each of us is solely responsible for our own words and actions.

A deeper, more nuanced, self-awareness-based conversation is needed when it comes to navigating internet relationships, power dynamics, and upholding responsibility. There are *absolutely* times, however, when calling a person out publicly feels like the *only option* to expose a person to their own problematic or abusive behavior and create enough impact in their life through reputational, financial, relational, or emotional damage to induce real change.

Callouts happen when boundaries feel crossed and either behavioral change or real reparations feel required. This is especially (and obviously) true in cases of abuse, illegal activity, racism, homophobia, or infringement of human rights. So many callout campaigns have aided in victims receiving justice. A poignant example is the #MeToo movement that allowed many women and assault survivors to receive justice and reparations for sexual violence. When millions of people came together for this global movement to share their stories, it sparked major social and legal changes, like destigmatizing and normalizing the conversation around sexual abuse and making it safer for survivors to come forward, publicly condemning many powerful men and people for their crimes, and providing legal defense for thousands of survivors.

For activism on both collective and individual scales, the ability to have a voice through social media and influence change is a massive win for society. Something we have yet to look at in the callout and cancellation conversations, however, is how little responsibility we assign to people doing the calling out. Often, righteousness and justified anger can snowball into an excuse to mistreat, dehumanize, disrespect, and exile people who may not deserve it.

Ask yourself this question: Would it be fair for someone to share your deepest, darkest, most tender moment when you weren't the best version of yourself with the public and put you on trial to determine whether or not you're a good person? You'd probably feel like your privacy was violated and that you were being unfairly judged for your darkest hour, your deepest ingrained patterns, and your most human mistakes that you've worked hard to not let define you.

When a person has a large platform and the resources to make these problems go away without actually taking proper accountability, it's a misuse of power. But these power dynamics can mirror internal challenges we may have with mistrusting authority, betrayal and powerlessness in past situations, unresolved mistreatment or disrespect, and other attachment-based behavior patterns. This is why taking a look inside of yourself through therapy, inner work, or even some of the exercises in this book can help you view these situations more objectively.

If you've been on the internet for any length of time, you've likely seen some callouts quickly escalate into harassment and lie spreading—causing a disproportionate amount of damage to the person being called out.

The lack of accountability for the commenters of internet conflicts opens a window for poor behavior that can leave a very negative impact on the person they're calling out. I've personally never seen more crude and hateful messages than I have from anonymous accounts. This inherent lack of accountability that comes from an anonymous account actually makes it very easy to project internal experiences, pain, and emotions onto others and spew it out to people. Think of it like having a bunch of balloons full of vomit weighing you down, and then seeing everyone else throwing their vomit balloons at someone who probably deserves it. You think, *Welp, I don't want these balloons full of vomit, even though they're mine. That person probably sucks—so, oh well!* We "project-ile" our own vomit onto other people without any proper way to stay accountable for our own behavior—and this is not okay.

People are getting canceled, called out, publicly shamed, harassed, and bullied for disagreements in views or beliefs. There can be a distinct lack of context and nuance about a given situation, and sometimes just existing "incorrectly" in the eyes of someone else can be seen as wrong. Some examples of this and its effects are:

- Public shaming of people leaving toxic religious communities and reclaiming their sexuality, which can re-trigger trauma or create feelings related to not belonging, being exiled, or being "wrong" for who you are.
- Hate accounts made about people who go from being vegan to eating meat for their health needs; in response, longtime friends distance themself from this person to avoid contamination by association. In making a personal decision, this person is alienated from a community to which they used to belong.

- Choosing to homeschool your children and using unconventional schooling practices because you feel it's in your children's best interests, only to be told you're an awful parent.
- People disagreeing on issues like parenting methods, religion, relationship styles, food choices, social causes, identities, and politics, causing harm to others by immediately deciding that whatever is different is wrong.
- Taking screenshots, messages, and conversations out of context and projecting individuals' judgments onto them—misconstruing the truth of a situation and spreading information that's ultimately incorrect.
- Being told your existence is not valid as an LGBTQIA+ person and getting publicly shamed and bashed online for simply existing as yourself authentically.

Callout and cancel culture has absolutely been a force for good for so many victims and communities who've been harmed and needed justice and reparation—and yet, there are still an incredible number of flaws in this system that need addressing if we are to minimize harm for everyone involved in these conflicts.

> "Freedom of speech does not mean freedom from accountability."
>
> @MX.DERAN

Walk a Mile in the Creator's Shoes

The moment your callout or cancellation story begins to circulate around the internet, there's no stopping the snowball effect. With every new stranger it reaches, there comes an onslaught of comments and messages. It'll be riddled with heightened emotion and opinions about you, even lies and rumors spread—and there's absolutely nothing you can do about it.

Most callouts and cancellation attempts leave the Creator feeling *entirely* helpless. If you start defending yourself, people will say you look guilty—a good person wouldn't have to tell the world they're a good person. And if you focus too heavily on yourself and not on what you're being called out for, people will point out you're doing it "wrong."

> Behind every account is a real person with feelings, struggles, and challenges we know nothing about.

The number of moves you can make without making the situation worse may seem limited. You have to wait it out, watching the fire spread across the internet. Maybe some of your colleagues unfollow you—or perhaps they get condemned for supporting and defending you. You're getting kicked off the island, exiled, and isolated. Whether this is occurring in a low-stakes way or a high-stakes way, the body will continue to feel activated, often to the point of hyperarousal and overwhelm of the nervous system.

In the body, you might experience feelings of hypervigilance to a perceived threat: stress, anxiety, extreme fear, shame, guilt . . . even if what's being said may not actually be true. The more some sort of message about you spreads, typically the more difficult it will be to avoid an emotional spiral. Sometimes, you might even begin to wonder if what people are saying holds some truth to it—questioning yourself exactly as they hope you will but through the lens of shame rather than curiosity.

If you happen to experience something akin to this without safe, supportive relationships and emotional-regulation tools, it's only natural to become overwhelmed or even potentially traumatized. Being told you're unwelcome and being put in the "irredeemable, bad person forever" box is horrible for anyone's mental health, no matter how strong you are. I consider myself a fairly regulated, grounded person with access to a vast amount of love, support, friendship, community, therapists, and healers—and I still found myself in an incredibly dark place during and after experiences of public callouts.

These kinds of experiences can turn nasty at any moment. Mob mentalities, heightened emotions, and "justice" often lead to direct messages becoming downright abusive. But the greater threat to pay attention to is the potential for re-traumatization. Re-traumatization is where you can experience a reactivation of wounds around being bullied, silenced, gaslit, harassed, or abused in your past. Truthfully, having a therapist or trusted support system on call is *imperative* if this ever occurs. I've seen people enter depressive states and heard of people committing suicide as a result of these kinds of public gang-ups.

> If you're having thoughts of suicide or feel in a state of distress or unsafety, call the National Suicide Prevention Lifeline at 1-800-273-8255.

On the other side of the coin, those who are doing the calling out often believe they are fully justified in doing so. Whatever the issue is, it's usually true that they have some sort of emotional connection to the topic or content. Perhaps they feel personally attacked by what a Creator said, or they feel like the Creator they're calling out is misusing their power or sharing misinformation. This experience can also be emotionally overwhelming and potentially re-traumatizing for both parties. Perhaps it feels similar to an unsafe situation from their past. Getting justice and speaking their piece may feel like the only option they have. Maybe you've been this person before—and knowing your target would likely read your messages allowed you to feel like you could impact change, and for a moment, you felt seen, valued, and validated. Below is an entry from my personal journal that I wrote in reflecting on my own painful experiences:

> When my pain is at its worst,
> my thoughts are at their ugliest.
> Remind yourself that your thoughts about a person
> or topic are a reflection of your
> unresolved pain in that area.
> It's the stories and interpretations we create of that pain
> that are not always accurate representations of reality.
> They are versions of it,
> but painted through the lens of your pain.

Shaming someone into action may get the job "done," but ultimately, it may reinforce that a person should hide a part of themselves because it is not welcome, which does not actually support true healing or lasting change. True healing requires a willingness to learn from our mistakes and grow through them. If we truly want a person to do this, they need to find the empowerment and humility within themselves to do so. When we put people in that "bad person" box, we tell them they are irredeemable. We reinforce that they can't make mistakes, that they are either at the top of the pedestal or belong on the floor. When someone apologizes and makes reparations but we refuse to take them out of that box, it affirms that they'll always be judged by their worst day. This isn't helpful or conducive to anyone's growth.

Think about a time you really hurt someone. A time you made a mistake. Now think about what happened after that. Did you get shamed, judged, or exiled? Or did the people around you hold space for your mistakes, recognize your humanity, and open their hearts with love while still standing for your growth? If the former, think about how different the outcome might've turned out had you experienced the support of the latter.

A New Perspective for How We Handle Conflict Online Between Creators and Audience Members

Each case of calling out, calling in, cancellation, or a smaller-scale disagreement has its own individual texture, which needs to be uniquely considered to determine how to handle it best. The biggest opportunity for the greater online community within the current social media landscape is to create personal accountability practices with ourselves and our own behavior during these situations. Both Creators and consumers can benefit from learning self-awareness, mindfulness, personal accountability, and reparative-action techniques to create a better online space for all.

Taking Responsibility as a Consumer

Calling out problematic behavior, advocating for change, and speaking up is your right. There's a comment box for a reason: it's a place for you to make a statement and stand up for what you believe in. But the next time you feel compelled to call someone out, ask yourself these questions (in any order):

- What can I take responsibility for first? Which feelings are mine?
- Can I process my experience with someone offline before taking it online?
- Where may I not be considering the humanity of the person I'm about to call out?
- What kind of courtesy would I want to receive if I were in their position?
- How can I be more loving?

Remember: you can only see a tiny part of any given situation. How sure are you that your positioning is actually true? The internet is written in pen, not pencil. Wrongfully canceling someone leaves a mark online that never gets erased—regardless of how true you genuinely believe something is. Be careful with the words you sling. There is a possibility you don't know the full story.

Behind each account is a real person living their own human experience and fighting internal fights you know nothing about. Rather than putting Creators on a pedestal, expecting perfection, see them as human beings who should be able to make mistakes from time to time. Of course, growing from mistakes and learning lessons is the ideal goal—but they cannot do that unless they see, acknowledge, and take responsibility for their actions. Are you providing them the dignity of their process?

If you believe someone is causing harm, try reaching out to them first. Share your observations, perspective, and experience. If they're not receptive to your reaching out, perhaps it's time to take it to your platform and tag them. If they're rude—hey, you've got a potential conflict on your hands. Is this your fight? What's your intention now? What is your ideal outcome? What standard of behavior do you want to hold yourself to? What are they triggering within you?

Taking Responsibility as a Creator

You may get called out once, twice, or multiple times in your career. Consumers may project onto you, judge you, or want to hold you accountable—and as unfair as it may be, it's okay. Having a public platform comes with a certain responsibility you probably didn't sign up for, but you do have it now. As the Spider-Man saying goes—*with great power comes great responsibility.* You're being watched, and your words and actions have impact. You don't have to be perfect, nor do you have to pretend you are. In fact, it's helpful for everyone if you regularly take the time to remind your audience that you're a flawed human figuring life out, too.

When someone judges you or calls you out, ask yourself:

- Is there any merit to what's being said?
- Is there a lesson I can learn from this situation?
- If hurt people hurt people, how may this commenter be hurting on the other side of the screen?
- How can I be more loving?

For all the stress they can cause you, public conflicts do have advantages. For one thing, they're an opportunity to show your audience a different point of view; for another, they allow you to model how other Creators can handle their own online conflicts. At a certain point in any debate (especially with a troll or hater), the goal isn't always to convince the person with whom you're arguing but rather to convince the people watching—the audience of people who *are* rooting for you. Who *do* want to see you win. Who have been supporting you and will continue to. If you can hold your own, create an airtight argument, take responsibility, and show emotional maturity, your audience will learn from you regardless of how the opposition ends up feeling.

Preparing Your Response to Getting Called Out

How you respond to your callout can either negatively or positively affect your brand and reputation. Just like in any relationship, how we show up during and after a conflict leaves an impact on how people relate to us, trust us, and judge us. We can't be expected to behave perfectly when we're triggered, unfairly judged, or publicly shamed—but if you can work toward more conscious and intentional public responses, it can actually become a wonderful opportunity to deepen trust with your followers. Ask yourself: Have you ever had a conflict with a friend or partner and ended up feeling closer to them as a result? If so, what were the factors that allowed that to happen? The resolution part likely included a genuine apology, genuine remorse, accountability, and reparative action. Here's how to prepare a thoughtful response to your callout that most benefits your reputation, brand, and trust with your followers:

Accept Responsibility and Say "Thank You"

Feeling attacked, judged, or criticized can make it extremely challenging to drop your ego and admit "defeat," but doing so shows a level of emotional maturity that will benefit both you and the other party. Accept responsibility for the things on your side of the street. It doesn't make you a bad person to make mistakes, miss a point, or have a lapse in judgment—it makes you a human being! We all have unconscious biases, so acknowledging how it's very possible you slipped up is a huge step in building trust. If someone spends more time blaming, deflecting, justifying, or minimizing than they do simply acknowledging that they might be in the wrong, it's usually a sign that they struggle to empathize and consider someone else's experience. When you say, "I can see how it could come across that way; thank you for pointing that out," it shows that you can consider multiple sides of a situation outside of your own.

Be Accountable and Repair the Damage

Depending on the severity of the situation, it's almost always beneficial to take accountability and make a statement about what you'll do to rectify or repair any damage done. This area is where many Creators find themselves needing to be performative and "say the right thing" or "follow the script" to get people off their backs. This is the point where you may need to do some inner exploration and excavation work to unpack what might actually be yours to take responsibility for. Refer back to chapter three on ego and remember: when you're trying to protect yourself or feel threatened, you might unconsciously make yourself superior ("I'm right, they're wrong," blame, justification as patterns), or inferior ("they're right, I must be wrong," people pleasing, over-responsibility, martyrdom, shame, guilt as patterns). A general rule with online relationships (or any relationship) is to work on finding the line between what's yours, and what's theirs. Take responsibility for your own emotional reactions, the places you acted unconsciously, or where your behavior may have caused harm (even unintentionally). But don't take on criticisms, judgments, or projections about who someone else thinks you should be, their view on morality and ethics that doesn't match up to yours, or anything that doesn't sit right with you.

If a troll is pissed you removed your breast implants, however, feel free to *not give a fuck and block them.* If an audience member got to see a new side of you when you reactively posted something petty about a person in your industry and now they don't totally trust you—you might find that there's more nuance there when it comes to a conversation.

If your behavior genuinely hurt someone or a large group of people—even if it was unintentional—create a sincere apology with remorse and action steps for the future woven in. This could look like taking a class on proper pronoun usage after misgendering someone. It could also look like acknowledging when a pattern of yours came out publicly, impacting your audience's sense of trust. It's also important that any proposed action steps are genuine and will be followed through. This is *not* a time to over-promise. Depending on the situation, you may want to do this privately through messages with the one or few people involved, or you might want to interact with your audience as a whole.

Practice discernment to determine what is and isn't yours to take responsibility for. Just because you made a mistake doesn't mean you deserve to be walked all over. The core of most conflict is due to a mismatch in expectations. If a consumer placed an expectation on you that you didn't agree to, that's a mismanaged expectation on their end. Stand up for what you believe is true and hold space for multiple perspectives, but don't carry a load that was never meant for you to carry.

On your platform, share one lesson you've learned from the situation and how you're going to take it into the next season of your life. An example could sound like "I've learned about how much more I could be adding trigger warnings to my content—so thank you to those who pointed that out. I appreciate the opportunity to learn and grow."

Clarify and Share the Context

In my most recent public callout about the prices of my business coaching, it was one full week of comments, messages, Reddit threads, and criticism videos. I found myself conflicted. Do I just let this happen and allow my work to speak for itself? Have I not done enough over the last years to prove my worth, credibility, and character?

I chose to use that moment to provide my current audience with some reassurance. It's natural to question people in positions of power, and I didn't want people who'd spent years trusting my word to start to wonder about my silence. So I spoke up. I reminded my audience of what my background is, the experience I have, and the results I've helped my clients achieve. I explained the value of business and life coaching to people who didn't understand it. I attempted to conduct myself as transparently and integrally as possible, mirroring to my audience who looks to me as a mentor how to handle themselves if this ever happened to them.

I received countless messages thanking me for showing up the way I did. Many of my audience members and past clients shared how triggering it was for them to watch someone like me—a person who has spent years working to help people, do my own inner work, and create as much safety in my spaces as possible—get misjudged like that so easily. It had scared many into shrinking or hiding themselves even further, ideally avoiding any similar situations.

You always have the right to clarify any incorrect, misconstrued, or taken-out-of-context statements. It's also perfectly okay to correct any flat-out lies. It doesn't mean you're avoiding responsibility—it means you're advocating for your right to set the facts straight. It's important to note that doing his can sometimes be quite overwhelming. Sharing information you perhaps never meant to share publicly (maybe about a relationship you wanted to keep private or a financial situation people were asking about) is forced vulnerability. This level of intimacy without a sense of safety can be a place where a lot of traumatic or emotionally upsetting situations can unravel for both audience members and Creators. If you ever find yourself in need of taking a step like this, it will be incredibly helpful to make sure you have some sort of support system—be it a therapist, trusted friend, or community—readily available.

A Final Note on Internet Conflict

Internet conflict can be messy, emotional, and sometimes unresolvable. Often, these situations can leave stains—whether on your reputation, your sense of comfort online, or in the hearts of the other people involved. In these moments, don't forget to stay connected to the people who have supported you and will continue to support you throughout conflicts. When you get called out, trolled, or judged, it can feel like everyone in the world thinks poorly of you, but that's completely untrue. Don't lose sight of those you've helped and who are rooting for you—especially those in your audience. Those are *your people*. Acknowledge and appreciate them at any opportunity you can.

During your next internet conflict, feel free to come back to this chapter so you can find and review ways to practice each of the principles. Ask yourself the important questions, set clear boundaries, be transparent, protect your peace, and consider the oppositional voices.

And remember: sometimes, a good old "*fuck the haters*" will do.

part three

part three
part three
part three

Building an Authentic Personal Brand

nine

The 9 Stages of Personal Branding

> "All of us need to understand the importance of branding. We are CEOs of our own companies: Me Inc. To be in business today, our most important job is to be head marketer for the brand called You."
>
> Tom Peters

A personal brand is what people think about when they talk about you. It's the story they tell when they share your content with a friend. It's the memory you imprint on their heart and minds because of your personality, your impact, and your . . . you-ness. Personal branding is an interesting journey because you're really figuring out: Who am I, and what is my brand? Who is Amanda Bucci, and what is the Amanda Bucci brand? That question is the very premise of this whole book because all of us Content Creators are actively working on building a brand identity, seeking ways to match it with our authentic self but also working to see ourselves as maybe more than we are—bigger, more known, more influential. But at the same time, you get to work through the places inside of yourself that don't feel worthy of being a brand, or are scared of being known, or don't feel ready for the responsibility of being influential. So along your journey of truly landing into your personal brand, you're going to go through some significant psychological and emotional development.

When researching the link between personal branding and psychological-development models, I looked at a few different leaders to bring this connection to life in a way that will help you feel seen in your experience. Abraham Maslow, an American psychologist, developed a theory of a *hierarchy of needs* based on human development and the stages one needs to go through in order to reach self-actualization—that is, reaching one's full potential. Maslow's hierarchy of needs suggests that people are motivated to fulfill basic physiological and safety needs before moving on to more advanced needs such as love and belonging. In his theory, self-actualization isn't guaranteed but is a final need to strive toward. Similarly, Erik Erikson, a German-American developmental psychologist, came up with his *stages of psychosocial development*, which consist of eight stages in a predetermined order from infancy to adulthood. The stages are hope, will, purpose, competence, fidelity, love, care, and wisdom. Within each stage, a person experiences a psychosocial crisis that can have a positive or negative outcome for personality development.

The *Graves Model* (also known as *Spiral Dynamics*) comes from the work of American psychologist Clare Graves. Graves had originally set out to validate Maslow's theory, but he died before he had the chance to publish his research, and it never gained popularity the way that Maslow's work did.[12] Spiral Dynamics consist of eight levels of psychological worldviews that humans operate from—each subsequent worldview upgrading in its development. Each view has its own values, goals, preoccupations, and steps to evolve into the next worldview. In writing this section of the book, I saw how similar the stages of Spiral Dynamics are to those of the journey of personal branding, and I knew it'd be helpful to blend these two concepts together.

Similar to the models of self-development, your personal-branding development journey may have felt a little clunky, like you've oscillated between multiple stages or even found yourself stuck in one stage for a long time. Take a look at the following nine stages of personal branding and allow yourself to see yourself in them while you gain even more clarity about what you can do to move forward. We'll look at each of the stages, including the common experiences, threats, and opportunities that arise in each one. Within each of these stages, there is a chance to redefine what your brand and presence mean to you on social media.

STAGE 1: AVOIDANCE

In 2014, I almost didn't start a YouTube channel because I didn't like the sound of my voice on video. I remember listening back to my first video—in which I was dolled up with fake eyelashes and hair extensions—and saying to myself, "Ick, maybe I'm not cut out for this." I didn't realize it at the time, but deep down, I didn't believe that I deserved to be in front of the camera. My life, as I judged it, was uneventful, uninteresting, and wholly unworthy of being recorded, let alone watched. Numerous narratives ran through my head, reasons why I shouldn't start a YouTube channel:

It's just not for me.
This isn't who I am!
No one will want to listen to me.
What if people judge me?

But something deep inside still pulled me in. I decided it was worth a shot. I mean, how many people would really watch, anyway? If nothing else, I knew I needed to do this to satisfy my own curiosity and heal that unhelpful narrative. In hindsight, I'm glad I didn't believe all of my thoughts and quit before I even started.

followed

In this Avoidance Stage, your brain and ego have the job of keeping you safe by holding you in environments you're most familiar with. Your world—up until this point—is made up of what you know and can expect, and in that lies familiarity, predictability, and a comforting sense of certainty. Social media represents the opposite of that—a world filled with uncertainties, unknowns, and no defined path to success. There's a world of new skills, habits, and practices you've never tried! It isn't until you can start to *not* believe your thoughts and confidently move through that sensation of diving into the complete unknown that you can transcend the Avoidance Stage.

In this stage, you might judge those who create on social media, saying that they're self-absorbed, narcissistic, or attention-seeking—when in reality, you really want to be a Content Creator but struggle to face your own insecurities around becoming one. This is what's called a *projection*—a mirror of an internal judgment of oneself projected onto other people as a way for the ego to not take responsibility. If instead you took responsibility for your own feelings, it would require you to acknowledge what's truly on the inside: the calling to be on social media and share yourself. By acknowledging this truth, you would have to process and move through those beliefs around what it means to be a Content Creator and recognize that you don't need to buy into them. Without taking ownership of this calling, you may live your life unfulfilled, consuming the content of others but never truly stepping into the ring yourself.

Creators' Experience of the Avoidance Stage

In the Avoidance Stage, Creators:

- Are critical of Content Creators
- Aren't sure how they could even start creating content
- Identify with being a non–Content Creator to the point of not being able to see past that identity
- Focus on the negative parts of being a Content Creator to stay safe and comfortable, not stepping into the ring

- Are frozen and stuck in inaction
- Post content sporadically and occasionally

Threats of the Avoidance Stage

On the scale of absolute hell, depression, and apathy (1) to absolute ecstatic bliss, joy, peace, and magic (10), I used to live my life between a 4 and 6. Everything was "fine." I went to restaurants I didn't really enjoy, worked jobs I didn't feel excited about, and had relationships that felt generally comfortable and safe. In my unconscious awareness to life, I accidentally created an environment that didn't challenge me in the slightest. I did what I knew I was decent at, played it safe, and worked to maintain a sense of peacefulness. I grew up quite privileged: a middle-class white family living in Rhode Island with two loving parents who showed me love and met my physical and emotional needs. Although I am so grateful for what I had growing up, I had very little emotional or psychological incentive to push myself outside of my comfort zone, which created a sense of complacency in life. It wasn't until my junior year of college that the Universe interfered, and one of my best friends (the spontaneous one in the group), Tori, said, "Let's move to LA for the summer!"

Without knowing if I could even get a job and make enough money to pay for rent—along with the internal pattern of remaining in my comfort zone—I originally said no. But Tori wouldn't take no for an answer—she was determined to go and find a way to get me to come with her. She researched and found a list of places where we could apply for jobs, which was a great way to help handle that objection of mine. We ended up finding work at a restaurant on the Venice Beach Boardwalk and arrived in May 2014 to spend the summer there. This moment was the catalyst for the rest of my life to break open. Over the next seven years, I opened myself up to experiences at levels 7, 8, 9, and 10, which were balanced by experiences at levels 1, 2, and 3. And I wouldn't have had it any other way.

The greatest threat of the Avoidance Stage is simply *not* saying yes, staying stuck in mediocrity and safety. It's *almost* more dangerous to stay in this stage than to reach a rock-bottom moment where you make the conscious choice to get yourself out of it—because the lack of polarizing experiences doesn't give you much of a pull or push to do something different.

Opportunities for Growth in the Avoidance Stage

In this stage, life is attempting to guide you to your next steps. It may feel intimidating to dive into social media when there are millions of other people with established brands already creating content, but that doesn't mean there isn't room for you to do the same. Remove the notion that you are too late, too old, or too anything to get started. Yes, there are skills to develop and a journey for you to embark on—and yes, you might be nervous to really own this next level of yourself. But as you step forward, you make a choice to really own the idea that you can, in fact, create anything you desire. You might not know it yet, but you *do* have untapped gifts and talents. Take action and slowly move forward, day by day, moment by moment. Lean into what feels the most natural to you and begin sharing your story, expertise, and energy. Be vulnerable. Be brave. Be courageous.

STAGE 2: CONSUMPTION CONFUSION

In the first few years of being a business coach, I worked with many Creators who were in the early stages of their brands and businesses. The challenge for so many of them was not having the knowledge, know-how, or skills of successful Content Creators. They'd reveal how much time and effort content creation was requiring of them and how directionless and scattered they felt trying to figure out what content was going to actually work. At that point in their journey, they weren't fully embodying and owning their inner Content Creator yet—and the next step was to view themselves as one. They mostly viewed themselves as content consumers who were inspired by their favorite Creators but not yet all the way "in the game." They were at the very beginning of the process of switching from "I'm a consumer, and I love the Creators

I follow" to "I'm a Creator with my own original ideas and thoughts." Once they made that shift, they were ready to start exploring and experimenting.

Consuming other people's content on social media is what the user does. Scrolling, watching, reading, and consuming is what the platform is created for, and what we consume on a daily basis heavily influences our perception of the world. As enjoyable and helpful as content consumption can be, it's also a very easy way to experience disconnection from yourself and your own inner creative voice. The more we consume and scroll, the easier it is to take on the ideas and energy of those whose content we consume. This is a form of not taking ownership of our own thoughts, ideas, and opinions and instead allowing those of others to become our own.

Creators' Experience of the Consumption-Confusion Stage

In the Consumption-Confusion Stage, Creators:

- Scroll through social media, with a small part of their brain reading and interpreting that information as content they could potentially create
- Feel paralyzed and overwhelmed by how much they don't know about content creation while consuming high-quality content
- Internalize not-good-enoughness as they try to figure out what to create
- Still relate to being on social media apps as a consumer rather than as a Content Creator

Threats of the Consumption-Confusion Stage

As humans, we tend to look outside of ourselves for answers—which is one of the biggest reasons we can feel so disconnected from ourselves and our purpose. The unconscious scrolling habits of social media consumers can be the catalyst for some of the greatest feelings of loneliness and disconnection in our modern world. Being alone and spending so much time consuming the content of other people, void of intention, keeps our brains extremely other-focused. Inherently, we compare ourselves to others—and, more specifically, it's a comparison to the success and highlight reels of others. But what you see online is only a very tiny percentage of who people truly are, what their lives are truly like, and what there is to know about them. In the unconsciousness of content consumption, following people without keeping what you see in perspective can shift you out of your internal experience. You may find yourself fixating onto the highlight reels of those whom you follow—distorting your sense of reality and leaving you feeling hopeless and lost.

Opportunities for Growth in the Consumption-Confusion Stage

In this external-projection experience, we see in others what we do not believe we have in ourselves. This can include characteristics like confidence, self-assurance, intelligence, beauty, poise, or humor. In psychology, this is called a positive projection. When we feel as though someone else has a positive quality that we don't, positive projection is a way for our ego to not take responsibility for claiming that quality and stay instead in the safe familiarity of our own mediocrity. To take full advantage of the opportunities for growth available in the Consumption-Confusion Stage, you *must* stop looking, scrolling, and consuming—and start creating.

Oftentimes, being so immersed in other people's content can stifle your own inner voice and creativity. As we mentioned in chapter two, creativity is a force that needs space to flow, and ideas for your own content will struggle to come in when your brain is full of other people. Unfollow and mute others as needed and clean up your social media habits so you can fully lean into your own vision and voice as a Creator. You can always go back to chapter two if you want additional support with that.

To ascend to the next level, ask yourself these questions:

- What qualities do I see in someone I follow that I do not believe I have in myself?
- If it were true that these are qualities I also have inside of me but haven't yet claimed, how would things have to change in my life?
- If I fully claimed ownership of these qualities, what would my next action step be?

STAGE 3: IMITATION

> "The urge, starting out, is to copy. And that's not a bad thing. Most of us only find our own voices after we've sounded like a lot of other people. But the one thing that you have that nobody else has is YOU. Your voice, your mind, your story, your vision. So write and draw and build and play and dance and live as only you can."
>
> NEIL GAIMAN, *THE VIEW FROM THE CHEAP SEATS*

In 2019, I was on a Zoom call with a business coaching client whose company was skyrocketing quickly, gaining momentum, and on track to reach that coveted seven-figure mark. Although this was a very exciting time for her, she found herself struggling with the kind of challenge you'd only face after boldly putting yourself out there and creating an impactful business. She noticed that one of her students who followed in her footsteps very closely seemed to be copying what she had done—step by step, and sometimes word for word. This person even took her exact course curriculum and used the same structure and titles for their own program.

In the world of content creation, many people's actions are fueled by a fear of being judged and a craving for external validation. In the Imitation Stage, the core threat is falling into the trap of believing that you have to be seen as perfect—and as quickly as possible. And it makes sense: there are *millions* of Content Creators out there absolutely crushing it, so it can be very vulnerable to still be learning how to create content in front of others. It can be tempting to co-opt other people's creative ideas and say, "Well, I could never do it better than they could—and they kill it!"

Making the decision to begin creating content on your own requires you to feel that "freshman in college" energy: vulnerable, new, and rapidly learning. It's normal to feel vulnerable or like an imposter whenever you're doing something new and different. Everyone has to work their way up as they develop skills. But in the social media world, this might be considered social suicide. In a frenzy of trying to bypass this stage and head straight toward the Full-Blown Branded Stage, many Creators try other Creators' ideas on for size. This includes content topics, frameworks, creative trends, captions, or tweets.

Creators' Experience of the Imitation Stage

In the Imitation Stage, Creators:

- Observe other people's caption structures, the way they film their videos, or the way they create their graphics and then utilize the same structures
- Repost other people's content (sometimes crediting them, sometimes not) and use it to build their own brand
- Sometimes plagiarize directly and steal people's exact content, presenting it as their own
- Hold onto beliefs that someone has done what they want to do so well that they couldn't possibly do it differently or better
- Experience overwhelm from feeling like their chosen industry is saturated and that everyone's already said everything worth saying
- Have a fear of being seen as a beginner, leading them to hide behind some sort of mask

Threats of the Imitation Stage

The greatest threat of this stage is behaving without integrity, allowing the fear of being seen as incompetent, not good enough, or imperfect overtake the truth of where you're at as a Creator: still learning and growing! As a society, we are conditioned to believe that we are "good" if we succeed in academics and sports, and our school systems reinforce this. Many kids have an additional critical eye on them with well-intentioned parents who are tough on them or other authority figures who hold high expectations. This can stick with children into adulthood, creating an internalized critical voice or a deeply rooted fear of being seen as imperfect, which can result in hiding one's own perceived imperfections. This kind of shame can linger and manifest in behaviors like plagiarizing or copying others and ultimately using a mask—protecting themselves from facing their fear. And although it's not our jobs (nor is it ethical) to pathologize someone who may have copied you as a way to make it make sense, it can be helpful to understand a bit of the psychology behind what could be happening.

Opportunities in the Imitation Stage

Pretend you're entering your freshman year of high school. Everyone knows you're new, and some people may bully you for it. Ultimately, it is an accepted fact that freshmen are new to the high-school hierarchy and will eventually turn into sophomores, juniors, and seniors. But they can't skip the lessons that come with being a freshman. There's so much to learn academically and socially, and even spending time walking the halls or sitting at lunch can provide them with the crucial learning lessons they *truly* need.

Becoming a Content Creator is similar. There is so much to learn—and creating content is a muscle to be strengthened. Assuming you'll be an epic Creator from the get-go is like assuming a baby will be good at walking on their first attempt. It just doesn't work like that. The greatest opportunity you can give yourself is permission to be in the learning phase and allow things to be messy. If you can adopt a sense of acceptance in this stage, a lot of those urges to act without integrity will subside. Say to yourself, "It's normal that I'm not the best at this right now—but I'm ready to learn and will use each piece of content I create as an opportunity to improve."

With this mindset in place, it is actually *very* helpful to utilize different content formats you see other people using, so long as you're not copying at a level that would feel disingenuous. Allow your inner integrity compass to guide you in your actions. There are hundreds of places from which you can obtain templates for graphics, follow certain trending formats on different platforms, or study other people's caption structures. This stage is definitely an opportunity—*if* you keep that student hat on.

Trying other people's content frameworks on for size is only natural. In fact, it's a way to see how you fit within those frameworks. You'll learn how to be more consistent and become more acquainted with your own creative expression in this stage. We all have the power to come up with our own creative ideas; we just have to trust that we are good enough to do so and give ourselves the time and space for ideas to flourish.

> Flip back to chapter two, "Embodying Your Inner Content Creator," for more tips on bringing your own inner, authentic creativity to life.

STAGE 4: AWARENESS

After the self-discovery process is underway, you may finally begin relating to your content as your own—rather than as a hodge-podge of other people's styles, voices, opinions, and content ideas. You are building more awareness of what you do and don't want to share online through self-observation and feedback. You're experimenting, testing, and reviewing the "data" as you walk along this new path. There's a lot of information coming at you, but you're taking it in stride and using that information to make more aligned content as you go.

Think of the Awareness Stage as *getting into the swing of things*. It's a place where you may feel as though you've found some level of footing. Yes, you still have plenty to learn—but you are moving forward with your own *content flavor* that feels more and more like you. You might notice which content pieces, topics, or angles connect most to your audience, which posts feel best for you, and which posts feel like you're creating out of obligation, lack, or fear.

followed

Creators' Experience of the Awareness Stage

In the Awareness Stage, Creators:

- Develop a better understanding of what kind of content they naturally enjoy creating
- Have a general idea of what to say (content) and how to say it (format/delivery)
- Try out different types of content—with some lack of cohesion but still within the realm of relevance
- Pay close attention to how other people respond to their content, using that information to get better

Threats of the Awareness Stage

The greatest threat of this stage is a sense of increased awareness of what you *don't* know (about your industry, niche, expertise, or Content Creator skills and roles), leading to a feeling of imposter syndrome. The *Dunning–Kruger effect* (based on work by Cornell University psychologists David Dunning and Justin Kruger in 1999) shows us that at low levels of knowledge, people often have an increased sense of confidence, almost to a fault. In other words, people who don't know very much about a subject will often feel like they're more of an expert than they truly are. Shortly afterwards, however, at a slightly higher level of knowledge, comes a huge dip in self-confidence. This is when someone realizes exactly how much they *don't* know—and confidence can drop dramatically (right before another upswing after gaining more experience and knowledge). It can be easy to fall into self-doubt, despair, and hopelessness in this stage. But don't give up: this is simply the beginning of your journey.

A secondary threat of the Awareness Stage comes from hyper-focusing on audience response, feedback, and analytics to the point where a Creator feels the need to make the majority of their content decisions based on what will perform best in terms of number of likes, comments, or views. This is a slippery slope, as there are multiple ways to interpret successful content outside of engagement metrics. Content does best when it's a combination of what you want to say and what your audience wants to hear.

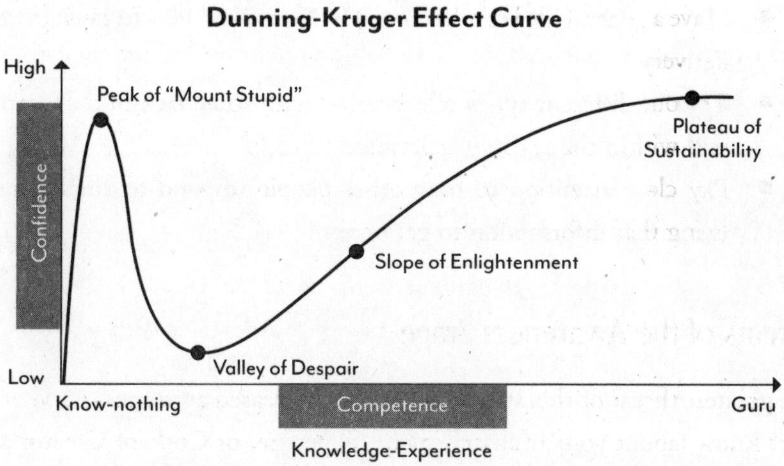

Opportunities in the Awareness Stage

The greatest opportunity of this stage is to learn how to interpret the information you're receiving from your social media account on all fronts—analytics, feedback, *and* feelings. In order to move into the Confidently Crushing Stage, it's not just about figuring out which content gets you the most followers but also about understanding which content feels best for you to create and will work well for your audience. I promise—there is a nice middle ground.

Expand your view of what "success" means for a piece of content. Yes, higher engagement, comments, and feedback are likely to give you information about what people want, but there are plenty of types of content that will most likely get low engagement *and* still support your brand positively. It doesn't have to be a case of each new post getting more likes than the previous one.

followed

For example: if you write a caption that makes people stop and think, they may press "Save" without commenting—but they are *absolutely* left impacted. If you post a carousel that triggers them, they may feel initial discomfort arise, but ultimately they could still go on to see that post as impactful, too. It may lead to growth and self-development, even if you don't see it personally. If you post a sales-related reel, it probably won't go viral—but it will increase your website clicks, which might lead to more customers, clients, and revenue.

Awareness Stage Reflection Exercise

Rate your last ten pieces of content on a scale of 1 to 10, with 1 being "least aligned with who I am" and 10 being "most aligned with who I am." Do you notice any trends or themes?

Next, rate your last ten pieces of content on a scale of 1 to 10, with 1 being "stayed comfortable in what I know" and 10 being "stretched me the most." Do you notice any trends or themes?

STAGE 5: CONFIDENTLY CRUSHING

You're in the pocket of flowing content creation because you've taken the time to learn what kind of content will best support your audience and blended that with the kind of content you want to create—without it feeling like those are two separate things. You understand your audience at a core level: the challenges they face, what they find entertaining, what they want more of from you, how you can help them grow, and how all of this helps *you* grow! You know what to do and how to do it in the Confidently Crushing Stage.

Creators' Experience of the Confidently Crushing Stage

In the Confidently Crushing Stage, Creators:

- Feel grounded in their ability to create content, reach the audience they desire, and achieve results in that process
- Have clarity and proficiency in their content-creation process, becoming more seamless by the day
- Are connected to their unique voice, knowing they have a place in their industry
- Post at a frequency that works for them
- Are on the up and up in their brand journey, reaching new goals and milestones

Threats of the Confidently Crushing Stage

Although there's a general sense of confidence in this stage, it doesn't mean that the Creator is exempt from their own personal patterns, ego- or fear-driven responses, and challenges that may be present. When you begin to feel confident as a Content Creator, the greatest internal threats are usually:

- **Comparison**: Hyperawareness of how you compare to other people in your space, usually with an ego-inflation ("I'm better than so-and-so because . . .") or ego-deflation ("I'm less than so-and-so because . . .") response in the mind.
- **Self-Judgment**: Judging the way you speak, write, or create. Judging the numbers and metrics you have. Judging how far along you are in your journey.
- **People-Pleasing**: Avoidance of being polarizing or disagreeable out of fear of judgment from others.

followed

- **Miscommunications or Ignorance**: Publicly speaking to a certain group of people while excluding others, or simply miscommunicating a point that ended up being harmful to someone or a group of people.
- **Imposter Syndrome:** Feeling like a fraud, unqualified to speak on a subject, even when this is factually untrue.
- **Complacency:** Wanting to stay comfortable with the level of visibility or success you have rather than taking the next step.

Opportunities in the Confidently Crushing Stage

To get to the Full-Blown Branded Stage, review how you're showing up in every area of your business and brand:

- Are you embodying the beliefs, ideas, behaviors, and identity you're teaching?
- Do what you say online and who you are in real life feel congruent?
- Have you set and enforced boundaries around your social media usage so you still feel energized to show up as your best self?
- Are you connected to your purpose, in the sense that you know what gifts you bring to the world? Are you actively sharing those gifts?
- Are you stepping into your power by choosing to do the thing that scares you but that you know is what you're supposed to do?

Answering these questions will help you uncover your inner *Full-Blown Creator*, taking you into the next stage of Personal Brand Development.

> Keep exploring, staying consistent, and extracting lessons about yourself and your audience during this stage. Your experiment is working; now it's time to refine.

STAGE 6: FULL-BLOWN BRANDED

One of my favorite things is to watch people go from hiding behind their content to being fully seen and showing up in their power online. One of my business clients recently did just that. Sam came to me with a social media page full of infographics and barely any images of herself. Now, opting for infographics over selfies doesn't automatically mean you're hiding, but for Sam it did—because that's what she told me.

Sam really wanted to work on feeling safe to be seen but had so many blocks around what that would mean. She dedicated an entire year to doing work around self-love, worthiness, people-pleasing, and fear—and now she makes Instagram Reels in her bikini *dancing* every other day. She brought so many more dimensions of herself and her personality online by posting photos, videos, stories, and Reels that come directly inspired by her soul. She went Full-Blown Branded.

The Full-Blown Branded Stage is the point you reach when you are not only confident in your abilities to create impactful content but also radiate a sense of being *fully embodied* in that brand. When you're in this stage, your audience can feel that who you are within your brand is exactly who you're meant to show up as. You're in a regular content-creation flow, creating what works well for your audience, and are being rewarded for it. Your level of connection to yourself as a person and a brand is gracefully intertwined. You've let the fullness of who you are shine online. You're living in integrity with your values as a Creator, posting only what is best for you and the people you're supporting. You may still have your own personal inner work to do to minimize fears and negative patterns, but you're ultimately aligned and thriving on a brand level.

Creators' Experience of the Full-Blown Branded Stage

In the Full-Blown Branded Stage, Creators:

- Share multiple parts of themselves and don't live in a sense of hiding online
- Are confident that what they're posting is what they need to be posting
- Are aware of where they fit within their industry and niche and proudly hold that position
- Grow their audience and business in an upward trajectory
- Experience self-love and worthiness of having all they desire

Threats of the Full-Blown Branded Stage

Behind the scenes, a Content Creator in this stage might be grappling with personal or emotional challenges or life changes that directly conflict with the brand they have. In the *shadow aspect* of this stage, the brand can become the *external persona* the Creator feels obligated to keep showing up for. During this stage, the external persona mostly matches who the Creator is as a person, but that doesn't exempt them from feeling pressure to keep it up. The early stages of the Plateau Stage may begin creeping through in moments of personal struggle or doubt.

Creators in this stage may struggle to:

- Maintain their integrity
- Set and enforce boundaries
- Be vulnerable or be seen imperfectly
- Release themselves from the pressure of being looked to as a role model
- Receive a lot of feedback about how they're being perceived
- Navigate experiences like being called out, canceled, judged, and criticized

Opportunities of the Full-Blown Branded Stage

Reaching success can leave your ego inflated, blinding you to the reality that you are not your Content Creator persona. Your true self is the one who experiences and witnesses it all. The greatest opportunity here is to not get caught up in the expectations of what it means to have "success." You are still a person with feelings, flaws, and growth ahead of you. That doesn't mean you aren't worthy or amazing (because you are!). It simply means that you still get to be a human and meet your own physical, emotional, and energetic needs. This may look like setting boundaries around your DM communication or being truthful when you inevitably make a mistake. This kind of humility will keep you grounded in your success.

> Let yourself feel good, enjoy the fruits of your labor, and soak it all in! But don't forget to remain curious with a student mindset.

STAGE 7: PLATEAU

One of my clients (let's call her Melanie) came to me in May 2021, extremely stuck with her fitness brand. People were unfollowing her left and right; clients kept canceling their contracts. It felt like every single thing she had been doing for years and *knew* to be successful was no longer working—and in fact was doing the actual *opposite* of what she wanted!

Her audience had been following her journey for so long and were now moving on in their own lives, no longer needing the content she was sharing about fat loss because they were on to the next phase of their health and fitness journey. Melanie thought that she could continue doing what had worked for her for years without changing anything and was nervous to confront the idea that it was time to innovate and upgrade her brand to keep up with changes in the market.

The antidote for Melanie was to see that she had some changes to make in her brand and content that more fully represented who she was and what she could teach her clients. She reinvented her brand, focusing more on stress management, hormone balance, and helping women in fitness move from rigidity to fluidity. This is the exact change her audience was *waiting* for her to make—and she went on to revive her brand and business within a few short weeks.

This is a stage many Content Creators hit after reaching their own Full-Blown Branded Stage—the Plateau Stage. We create so much content for our audiences that it can eventually feel like we've spoken about the same topics for years. Sometimes, if we're coasting along in that, our engagement can start to take a dip. If you've been at the Full-Blown Branded Stage and are determined that you've found the formula that works for you, and all of a sudden, it stops working—what do you do? It's an indicator that you may be entering the Plateau Stage.

This is the stage that calls for you to reflect on your brand by taking a step back, reviewing where you've been, and actively deciding where you want to take things. That might look like going deeper on the same topics, hopping along with new trends, enhancing your writing skills, expanding your education, or shifting your niche all together. Rather than falling into the trap of trying to keep up and stay relevant, this is an opportunity to redefine yourself and your brand.

Creators' Experience of the Plateau Stage

In the Plateau Stage, Creators:

- Create the same kind of content they've created for years, clinging to what once worked

- Avoid looking at the parts of themselves they aren't bringing online, as they are so used to experiencing success without needing to try anything new or change
- Feel imposter syndrome and self-doubt about their identity
- Are possibly disconnected from the journey their audience and community are on, as they are focused on keeping their account the same without attuning to those around them

Threats of the Plateau Stage

Creators in this stage may be at risk of falling into a personal brand crisis, which can include losing followers, confidence, and momentum. They may feel powerless to the ever-changing algorithm or feel confused about how to get back on track. When the strategies that once worked no longer work and engagement starts decreasing, it can feel confusing. What gives, right?! Without the proper tools and awareness, Creators may experience a challenging identity crisis that will have them questioning themselves, their worth, and their money-making potential. This may activate projection and anger from within, which can potentially spill onto a platform and even unintentionally come through in conversations with audience members. Creators in the Plateau Stage might experience:

- Feeling like a victim or a lack of power
- Frustration and confusion with the algorithm
- Resistance to change
- Denial or anger about all of the above
- Pressure to stay relevant

Opportunities in the Plateau Stage

The opportunities of this stage are great—and often come at the tail end of the inevitable identity crisis. We will dive deeper into this in chapter eleven,

"Pivoting Powerfully," but the best thing to do is to accept this new reality and look inside *yourself* for the answers. I've pivoted many times in my career (along with helping countless Creators do the same). The answer never lies in trying to hack the algorithm or in someone else's YouTube video—or even in this book. It's about recognizing that you—as a person—have changed and that your brand hasn't yet caught up to those changes.

The moment you accept that it's time to reinvent yourself, you are on the precipice of transformation. You're bravely stepping into claiming and owning even more of who you are, which will fill you with empowerment, excitement, and energy to create more.

> There are many moments in life where it's important to go inward and allow the cocoon to hold and nurture us while we allow the shifts in our life to happen. This slowing down to pause doesn't always get the same response or reaction as when we're doing well, posting frequently, and in a creative flow, but it's just as important as any other season.

STAGE 8: REINVENTION

In my time primarily working as a business coach, I saw that there were so many avenues to take my brand through within that world. I could double down on marketing and copywriting, or focus on leadership and scaling, or focus on social media and visibility. But what I found myself the most interested in whenever I'd work with clients was always what they were feeling and experiencing while they were growing their businesses—not the business mechanics themselves. And as much as I resisted yet another pivot, it was undeniable that I was better suited to brand myself as a life and leadership coach rather than a business coach. I could talk about business, but I also wanted to talk about the underlying healing work people were doing through their businesses, their relationships, and even more aspects of their life. So in 2022—for the third time in my career—I found myself in the Reinvention Stage.

The Reinvention Stage is a natural result of taking full advantage of the opportunities in the Plateau Stage. In your personal-branding development, there is a natural point where you'll feel the need to shift the way you've been doing things—whether that's changing from pictures to infographics or switching entire industries.

In this stage, Creators are ready to leave the predictability of the Full-Blown Branded and Plateau Stages and *reinvent themselves by making a pivot.* The Creator experiences an internal, personal change—and in order to have their external brand match their internal reality, they need to make an adjustment to their content, brand strategy, and/or direction.

I have worked with so many entrepreneurs and online content creators who have experienced that strange sensation of realizing they can either continue doubling down on the brand they've already built—even if it doesn't fully represent who they are today—or continue shifting their content, brand, and even offerings and businesses to match the person they've become.

Creators' Experience of the Reinvention Stage:

In the Reinvention Stage, Creators:

- Feel an overwhelming sense of not being able to go back to their "old self," as scary as it is to step into their "new self"
- Start creating content in a different way for the first time
- Navigate the challenges of some of their followers not being on board with this change, unfollowing them, or feeling upset that their content has shifted

- May experience extreme imposter syndrome and self-doubt as they so publicly go through stages 3–6 of the 9 Stages of Personal Branding all over again
- Have a sense of excitement for this process with a newfound sense of creative energy pulsing through them

Threats of the Reinvention Stage

The greatest threat during this stage is a lack of confidence in being seen as the student, protecting yourself from vulnerability by projecting an air of authority. One of the greatest challenges of our time for Content Creators is that being in the public eye (no matter how big or small your audience) can leave you feeling like you're being constantly watched—so you better not fuck up. With that, there's a fine line between educating people as an expert and educating people as a student. The journey to becoming an "expert" is nonlinear. In chapter eleven, which discusses pivoting, I'll share how long it truly takes to become fully embodied in your new message. For now, I'll just say this: *fully embrace being a student.* Be honest about what you're learning, remain humble in your studies, give credit where credit is due, and admit when you are wrong.

Opportunities in the Reinvention Stage

There are three pathways available once you reach the Reinvention Stage. You can either:

1. **Keep growing into your current space, expanding your brand in different ways.** You may stay at the same level of knowledge and expertise, but you just take that brand and bring it into new spaces. You can do this by:
   a. Adding on a new platform
   b. Adding one or many new offers

c. Collaborating with others in your industry
d. Getting PR and increasing your visibility across platforms

2. **Take your expertise and brand deeper.** You can gain more expertise and go deeper into the mastery of your current niche. This will enhance your level of credibility within your space. This is for you if you feel very strongly about your current niche, and are noticing how interested you are in learning about a specific area of your niche and going down that path. We'll talk about this in the next chapter.
3. **Pivot into a different industry, niche, or level of your personal brand.** You can do this by starting to share content with a different topic or theme. Read more about this process in chapter eleven, "Pivoting Powerfully."

STAGE 9: TRANSCENDENCE

In May of 2018, I went through what some call a spiritual awakening, which is an experience where you "wake up" to your own internal patterns and begin to see the places in your life where you're not actually living as who you truly are—but instead through a combination of trauma responses and societal conditions and norms. This experience felt like I was on a rocket ship of personal growth and development for three years straight. I went to spiritual workshops, attended therapy, devoured self-help books, binge-listened to podcasts, and learned meditation, breathwork, and ecstatic dance. I sat in multiple psychedelic journeys and even attended the University of Santa Monica to formally study spiritual psychology.

All of this occurred while being in the public eye, in front of my audience. This deep pivot within myself activated a deep pivot within my brand—which ultimately reflected in my metrics and analytics. The more I posted polarizing content about consciousness and spirituality, the more audience members who followed me in the early days for booty workouts and bodybuilding pics fell to the wayside. Over the course of a few years, I watched my follower count continue to dip—losing a few hundred followers a week.

In healing from people-pleasing, I knew that the discomfort I felt knowing the public was watching me lose followers was not a good enough reason to abandon myself and avoid talking about the ideas and topics I felt called to share. The consequences of always trying to please others were too great for me to bear anymore, so I chose to live authentically on my platform—regardless of the fact that my likes and followers were publicly decreasing. Interestingly enough, I actually *gained* hundreds of new followers a week as well, but the loss happened faster than the gain, so even though I knew I'd gained 100,000 followers with my new pivot, losing 120,000 felt bigger.

I've seen these kinds of follower losses have an extremely large mental and emotional impact on influencers, business owners, and Content Creators. Gaining followers—no matter how many—gives our bodies a rush of dopamine and inflates our egos. This phenomenon creates an anchor inside us that says, "This particular brand identity is lovable, worthy, and valued in this society. Do all that you can not to lose it." So we keep feeding the beast—gaining more followers, getting that dopamine, and anchoring in this identity of someone the world sees as valuable. All humans are encoded with the basic human need to feel worthy and valuable, and depending on your childhood, upbringing, and traumatic history, feeling valued in the world can be directly correlated in your psyche to being safe. Having that sense of safety start to go away can feel like a major threat, likely causing some major nervous-system dysregulation.

In the Transcendence Stage, you will at some point experience a sense of *identity death*: death of the part of yourself that attached your self-worth and value to your followers, what other people think of you, and your social media platform altogether. The intention of this stage is to support you in separating your identity and self-worth from your social media presence and to remind you that you don't need to do or be anything to be inherently worthy. You are worthy because you are.

Creators' Experience of the Transcendence Stage

In the Transcendence Stage, Creators:

- Work to heal childhood wounds and patterns affecting their social media experience
- Decide their posting schedule and content based on what feels right for them, not what they think they "should" do
- Can take projections, trolls, haters, and critics with a grain of salt and have a level of objectivity and separation from them
- Can experience shifts in their brand and online presence and acknowledge that they aren't a threat to their success

Threats of the Transcendence Stage

The greatest threat of the Transcendence Stage is the threat to the ego's desire to continue achieving and accomplishing so it can continue to feel fed through validation. You may experience some discomfort or fear around letting go of posting every single day, making posts that cause people to unfollow you, or taking a social media detox. Any one of these actions will be in direct opposition to the way your psyche developed as a Content Creator dependent on the validation and approval of others.

Opportunities of the Transcendence Stage

This is one of the most beautiful stages of your journey as a Content Creator—liberating yourself from not only the oppressive forces of the platforms you use but also the parts of your psyche that were keeping you suffering and stressed. This process may seem challenging, but the greatest tool you have is your own awareness and observation. Remind yourself: *I am not my thoughts or feelings; I am the observer of those thoughts and feelings.* As old patterns or narratives arise, observe your thoughts and bodily sensations. You are witnessing neural pathways that have been grooved over and over again for possibly years, forming habits and automated behavior sets that require conscious awareness, slowing down, and some mindful and intentional action to change. Don't worry—it's all more than possible. You can be yourself on social media, free from the stresses or pressures of needing to be someone for everyone else. You can just be yourself, run your account, and follow strategies to grow—without feeling obligated or constrained in the process.

■ ■ ■

Let this chapter serve as a guide to help what's happening inside and around you make a little more sense. Each of these stages has its own lessons and wisdom for you to extract, so ask yourself: What growth is available to me next? How can my personal brand consistently evolve to suit both my desires and my evolution?

ten

Niching Down into Yourself

"Ask Me Anything! Self-Awareness. Psychedelics. Navigating Relationships. Aligned Business. Being Authentic. Energetics. Conscious Marketing. Poly/Sex."

"**Ask Me Anything!** Being Vegan. Interior Decorating. Parenting Toddlers. Where to Get the Best Furniture. Vegan Recipes. Living in Oklahoma."

"**Ask Me Anything!** Exercise. Hair Stuff. Step Challenge. Special-Needs Kids. Dieting. Time Management. Business Coaching."

These are all Instagram Stories slides of different Creators hosting Q&As for their audiences. Out of context, each of these sets seems like a strange grab bag of topics. Given their variety, they don't fit into the neat little box the marketing world calls a *niche.* Except that they *aren't* random—they're different elements of the lives of these respective Creators, each one a multidimensional, complex human being who wants to speak about different topics.

Marketing has taught Creators and entrepreneurs to "niche down" in order to succeed—in other words, to pick an industry, find a specialty within that industry, target an ideal audience, and focus on creating content and solving problems for that group of people. The process of establishing your brand within a niche includes identifying your experiences, interests, passions, and skills—and then creating content, offers, and products for your target market from that position. So what happens when you've got many different interests and passions you want to share with your audience? How do you choose without feeling like you have to pick one thing forever without changing to succeed? And how can you avoid pigeonholing yourself so you can be free to do what you want in the future?

Picking a singular niche provides a level of simplicity, focus, and clarity that lends itself to an easier, swifter process reaching your goals. This is the difference between "I help people lose fat and gain confidence" and "I help high-achieving corporate moms increase their energy through intermittent fasting and HIIT workouts." My first niche that I accidentally found myself in was bodybuilding—which is an extremely specific form of fitness filled with things like zero-calorie dressings, over-the-top exercise regimes, and people who remain loyal to a particular activewear brand. Niching claims that the more specific you get with who you're targeting with your content and what you're offering them, the easier it is to become well-known as a leader in that area. There's something really appealing when you know *exactly* what you're going to get from someone you follow—recipe videos, life advice, dance TikToks, comedy reels, or travel vlogs. That kind of clarity also provides each Creator a simple, formulaic structure from which to create. Once you find a flow for the kind of content that works for you, you can keep making it—refining it, improving it, adding products to it—and grow in a fairly linear fashion. When it comes to marketing efficiency, picking a niche is sound advice.

And yet, for many of you, reading about traditional niching makes your soul cringe. This standard version of niching directly conflicts with your free-spirited nature and desire to be expressed as a whole human being rather than a fragment of yourself. And I'll tell you right now—you are not alone, as the deeper human desire to be seen and accepted for all of who we are is the root of why so many Creators rebel against the idea of traditional niching. Because marketing is rooted in human psychology, we must address the inherent limitations in marketing methods as a tool set. As we evolve and grow as people, we have more to say about a greater number of topics. With regard to content as an outward expression of personal experience, cleaving to narrowly defined borders of what's allowable within a niche isn't just constraining; it's shortsighted. Creators have already begun breaking apart the notion of a singular niche by finding strategic ways to share multiple things at once—and that rebellious act is what I call *niching down into yourself.*

In my journey as a Content Creator, I've written about bodybuilding, nutrition, powerlifting, body image, mental health, entrepreneurship, marketing, social media, money, creativity, spirituality, trauma healing, subconscious reprogramming, psychology, energetics, conscious communication, relationships, sexuality, and leadership. That doesn't resemble anything close to one specific niche, but it does represent me and my relentless curiosity for the nature of humanity. Along the way, I've existed in the Bodybuilding Fitness Influencer Niche, and then the Build Your Business as a Fitness Coach Niche, and then the Build Your Business as a Spiritual Entrepreneur Niche. Now I feel like I'm in the Spiritual Entrepreneur, Polyamorous, Psychedelics, Neurodivergent, Energetic, Witch, and Communication Niche. You could call that life coaching, to distill it into an elevator pitch. In allowing space for all of these parts of myself to come online and be included in my brand, my own unique niche formed itself. The Amanda Bucci Niche. The niche that only I can occupy. You have your own unique niche, too.

If picking one niche is focusing on one core topic and becoming well-known for that, niching down into yourself is sharing the unique and multidimensional details of your personality, perspective, expression, and core essence—and trusting that combination to be specific enough to attract the exact audience of people who resonate with it. It's allowing yourself to be seen in your evolution as a person and a brand, letting people meet you there. It's knowing that you don't need to fragment yourself as a Content Creator in order to be successful and that you can find a way to include and express the elements of you that feel like they should be seen online.

> You are the niche. Following your fascinations, creating content that's rooted in your expertise and personal story, and then bringing all of your quirks and other interests to the table ultimately creates your own unique niche that no one else exists in.

If you don't feel stifled by having a single-topic niche—this is not an invitation to complicate the simple and clear brand that's working for you right now. This is just an opportunity to view your brand as something that is free to evolve with you. Right now, the brand of "you" might represent one core topic or have one smashingly successful business—but what about your life ten years from now? Twenty years from now? Thirty years? If you think you'll still be posting about the same topics in 2053, more power to you. But on the off chance that you do find yourself called to explore speaking on or creating other kinds of content and expand what gets to feel included in your brand, remember: you *are* the niche.

Within the niching-down-into-yourself framework, begin to view those "out of the box" parts of yourself as the exact best ingredients of your brand that allow it to stand out from the crowd in a saturated market. Think about it this way: there are millions of people in thousands of niches right now, saying the same things over and over, trying to figure out how to grow their brand when everyone seems to look and sound the same. When there seems to be nothing new under the sun, the only *true differentiator* is the innovation of the person from which the content is delivered.

For years, I've been hosting group business coaching programs where anywhere between fifteen and forty online coaches and entrepreneurs gather to learn and grow for a season together. In the earlier stages of my coaching practice, I found that my clients consisted primarily of online fitness and business coaches who had similar business models. But even in my very first group, all illusions of similarity shattered when each coach shared and expressed their unique story, philosophies, values, methods, and texture of how and why they coach. Although they have fallen under the same niche, they each had their own unique flavor and energy to bring to the table. And as the years passed, I saw the entire industry evolve as coaching businesses became more refined and specific.

One of my clients, "Jess," had a large business coaching company that primarily served experienced fitness professionals. At the same time I was working with her, I had another client, "Erica," who was also a business coach. She, too, worked with fitness trainers, but she found herself attracting clients who were just starting their careers and needed help building basic business structures. Although both Jess and Erica were working with clients in the same industry, they each had totally different life paths, experiences, values, and needs—making each one better suited to helping a particular population within that industry and speaking to those specific subsets through their content. Over time, as Jess and Erica continued serving their respective audiences, their messaging (which at one point had many similarities) diverged to suit their brands. Each had its own texture and educational style. Most importantly, their audiences shifted in response, going through cycles of culling and curation as followers selected the message that felt most resonant.

Have you ever recognized how powerful it is when you deeply resonate with a Content Creator you follow? Something about the combination of their words, tone of voice, style of creating, place of residence, age, culture, life story, sense of humor, color and font choices, and energy *work* for you. That's not an accident—it's the magic of embodying your fullest expression as a Creator. The more we all seek to bring our full, authentic selves online, the more everyone will find the right people to serve, entertain, and influence them on their journey. There are a million options for which content we can consume, but every one of us is choosing to follow the Creators who resonate with those nuanced and specific versions of our humanity. This version of niching is still specific but can hold more of you at once.

THE PRINCIPLES OF NICHING DOWN INTO YOURSELF

So if niching down into yourself gives you free rein to be anyone and anything you desire—how can you still focus your brand in a way that's still successful? What's the process for creating a brand that captivates, magnetizes, and connects with the right people for you without it feeling like your content's all over the place? Is it possible to speak about being a parent, using psychedelics, navigating health and hormonal challenges, and your sexuality all in one fell swoop? With a little thoughtfulness and a bird's-eye-view perspective, it is. Let's review the principles of niching down into yourself as guidelines to consider when you're working to clarify your brand in a way that's not limiting, but expansive.

Principle 1: Your Core Essence Is the Umbrella of Your Brand

In the traditional marketing version of niching, you create a narrow focus of your brand by going from your industry to a subniche of that industry, then into a specific target demographic of people you want to serve, and then into a specific problem you solve for them. This could look like being a travel influencer for women who want to live nomadic lifestyles while feeling safe. You're in the travel industry, primarily supporting women, and helping them feel safer during their travels with your helpful suggestions. Of course, you might find that you want to branch out of this niche eventually, creating that same problem outlined earlier of needing to change up your brand and convince people to come along for a totally new ride with you.

Consider that your core value as a Content Creator is not actually in the tips you provide, the methods you use, or even the industry you're a part of but rather in your point of view, your core essence, your artistry, and the part of you that remains tried and true throughout any brand adjustment you might make. So even if you're no longer a travel influencer, if you've always found it really important to stay connected to your audience, introduce them to one another, build community, or share insights only you can share, people will still follow you simply because it's you they've always felt.

You might not know what your core essence is—because it's so inherently you, it can be difficult to see from the inside looking out. Your core essence is wrapped up in the way you do that extra zoom on your videos or the style you write in that makes people laugh. It's the way you develop your memes and how people know it's yours immediately once they see it. It's the tone of your voice—whether it's boisterous and silly or soft-spoken and gentle. It's your perspective on any topic—how you share your opinion, tell a story, or put a unique spin on something that's been created a hundred times already. It's not just *what* you create but *how* you create it.

Recently, I was thinking about what it looks like when I feel most confident in myself as a Creator, and it's never those moments when I'm projecting my voice loudly at the camera, screaming my message from the rooftops. For me personally, my confidence comes from the moments when my voice is a little lower and deeper, compelling my audience to listen closely, allowing my words to land in their hearts like a gentle, firm hug. My core essence isn't the most simple and easy to understand—because it's really for the people who enjoy that deeper, intuitive, thought-provoking message my brand provides.

Ask yourself: What is pure "me-ness"? When people come to my social media spaces, what do I want them to feel? Which parts of me do I want them to connect with? What do I want to be known for? What does it look like when I'm serving my specific flavor of "me" in my content? Throughout all the time I've been on social media, what has been a constant in what I share? Head to followedbook.io to answer these journaling questions for yourself, and watch how your brand awareness all begins to make more sense.

Principle 2: Your Most Authentic Content Will Be *Magnetic* to the Right People and *Repellent* to the Wrong People

One of the biggest concerns you might have along your journey is alienating or repelling some people by being too specific. You may often even feel a subtle awareness of the things people might say if you were to speak about something that feels true to you and your brand. Maybe you're religious but plan to speak about your sex life online—knowing that you might receive comments that mirror the critical and judgmental voice of your family. Perhaps you've always come across as a really nice, pleasant person but want to say something more direct and cheeky.

Although you might need to grapple with some people who will be repelled by the kind of content that feels most authentic to you, you'll very quickly notice that it will also magnetize the right people. Your brand will go from generic to memorable. More members of your audience will feel an emotional connection with what you do or say, creating a deeper connection between you and them. It allows people the opportunity to continue opting into an experience they genuinely want more of or to opt out of something they genuinely do not desire.

Remember: repelling people isn't a bad thing. Maybe a follower isn't at the stage of their life where they connect with empty-nesting or buying a home, or perhaps what you're sharing about money activates someone's own discontent with their relationship with their own finances. Some people just may not be interested in your passion for eco-friendly clothing, or they might find your political posts too confronting for their tastes. Some of your followers might have been there for the bikini selfies but not for the nuanced conversation around body image.

When you focus on being the fullest expression of your brand, people who are a clear "no" will leave or unfollow, and people who are a clear "yes" will:

- Be able to find you more easily
- Become advocates for your brand

- Feel like soulmate clients or customers
- Let you know how much you are impacting them

Principle 3: Find Your Unique Social Media Voice Through Digital Mediums

Have you ever felt like everyone in your industry was doing and saying all the same things—and no one was creating what you feel like creating? That's your innovative brand artist coming online, realizing that you have the perspective and power to represent something different in your space. When you're a Creator in an industry with thousands of others, it can feel like everyone is in competition with you, repeating similar trends and trying to "get theirs." But your inner creative genius might begin to feel frustrated and uninspired with what's going on, or like there's a whole part of the conversation lacking. The very moment you realize that you are the person to bring that conversation, style, or innovative idea forward is when you lead a whole new shift in your industry.

The traditional marketing principles you'll read about will usually tell you to discover your own competitive advantage, unique selling propositions, brand positioning, and "edge" that allows you to stay connected to your audience and attain success without getting lost in the sea of others just like you. Niching down into yourself is something similar but with a small twist: your unique selling proposition is *your unique perspective* on the same content and trends you see over and over. What matters is often not the information but the representation, interpretation, and person from which it comes. Sometimes, people just want to hear something from you, specifically.

How can you innovate in a small or big way on the same thing you've seen over and over? What unspoken thing is your industry not addressing, and how can you be the person to say it loudly and proudly? Or how can you say the same things but even better than others do—with backed-up research, embodied wisdom, and mastery in your communication?

Beyond that, how can you use different digital features to your advantage by using them as tools to develop your voice? How you choose to take pictures and express yourself in a photo shoot is entirely up to you. The style of microphone you use to record your YouTube videos and live streams is your choice. The way you conduct an interview for your podcast is your own form of artistry. Perhaps you've spent years writing articles and posts on Facebook and felt hesitant when TikTok was released—but once you tried it, you noticed that a funny, lighter version of yourself was able to come out. Or maybe you began your social media journey on YouTube, staying true to the format of long-form vlogging for years, doubling down on that because it's always allowed you to thrive as a Creator. Maybe you love making content about a particular topic but want to remain anonymous—so memes are the way to go, blending your energetic presence perfectly with humor and wit. You may be the person who feels uncomfortable on popular visual platforms, but podcasts are a place where you feel you can truly be yourself, engage with others through interviews, and explore the vast world of audio-only content.

When you start to play around with different features, tools, and apps to enhance and optimize your creations, it becomes this fun game of figuring out what draws you in the most. As you experiment and explore different content platforms, styles, and features, you might find new and creative parts of yourself you weren't even sure you had.

Principle 4: Bring People Along for Your Evolution

When you think back on your brand story thus far, ask yourself: What have been some of the most pivotal moments that have really shaped and defined your brand? For many Creators, those are the moments where they made a change or adjustment to how they created content based on a shift in their life at that time. Even if you haven't shared every part of your life with your audience, the things that happen in our lives influence the kind of content we lean into creating. Some life transitions that may affect how you run your content include:

- Marriage, breakups or divorce, having or adopting a child, or some other family transition
- Moving to a new location and being in a different environment
- Developing a new interest or passion
- A change in career or starting a new business venture
- Health issues, injuries, or other life-altering experiences
- Feeling bored or losing passion for the topic you've been creating content about
- Other deep personal challenges that affect all parts of your life
- Negative experiences on social media that leave you feeling uncomfortable or unsafe when being on one or more platforms

I cannot tell you how many clients I've coached through changing their Instagram handles. Each client had such an emotional process coming to terms with announcing their "new self" to the world. I've watched so many clients and friends change their handles from something with a defining niche word (like "fit," "health," "spiritual," or "biz") to their own personal name. Have you ever changed your brand name on social media? That moment was likely *iconic* for you! The day I went from @amandabuccifit to @amandabucci was a moment I will never forget. Bring people along for your evolution, as those pivotal moments will become defining pillars for your brand story.

YOU ARE THE NICHE

If I've learned one thing from coaching hundreds of clients in figuring out their niche, it's that the process of trying to help other people understand you is deeply personal. Whether it's changing your social media brand name or deciding to switch up your graphics, attempting to capture your essence in digital format is like trying to describe why you are the way you are. You are ineffable—and a niche, a brand, and content can never fully do you justice. But your absolute best attempts to express yourself through a brand is a self-development journey in and of itself. Whenever I'm working with a client on clarifying their brand, there always comes this beautiful moment when they realize there's a new, unexpressed, refined part of themself they'd like to share with their audience, even if that means rocking the boat of their preconceived brand. But finding a way to allow that part to be seen—whether it's an untold story shared on a podcast or a side of themself that can only get shared through audio—is what everyone's looking for. On the surface, we strategize on how to go about making new upgrades to our brand, but on a personal level, it's really about accepting more of who we are and proudly sharing that in front of a digital room full of people.

In the next chapter, we'll be looking at *pivoting*—another powerful process that can allow your personal brand to reflect who and where you are in your life. It's especially useful if you have made major life changes or want to reflect new or different parts of who you are that may seem like a major departure from your current content and brand. You'll see how to do this in a way that seems easy and effortless.

eleven

Pivoting Powerfully

> "You gotta keep changing. I'd rather keep changing and lose a lot of people along the way. I'm convinced that what sells, what I do, and who I am are completely different things, and if they meet—beautiful."
>
> —Neil Strauss

In May of 2018, I flew from Los Angeles to New York to record a pod-cast with social media magnate Gary Vaynerchuk. Loud, brash, and brilliant, Vaynerchuk is one of the most well-known entrepreneurs to have created and amplified success through prolific content creation. His famously frenetic mannerisms and candid speech stand out in stark contrast to most businesspeople, and in the hour we spent together, we found ourselves in agreement on the importance of pivoting.

Born in 1975 in Belarus (then still part of the Soviet Union, which would itself collapse a decade and a half later), Vaynerchuk arrived in the

States at three years old not speaking a word of English. But, to hear him tell it, once he learned to speak, he never stopped talking. You can hear him on thousands of podcast episodes, see him in tens of thousands of videos, or read his words in hundreds of thousands of social media posts or in any of his books—all of which have debuted on the *New York Times* bestseller list.

A lifelong hustler with an entrepreneurial bent whose early businesses included buying and reselling baseball cards, he had little interest in schooling or traditional work. But at fourteen, he was taken in hand by his father and forced to spend his nights and weekends working in the family liquor store. Though resistant at first, he flourished in the role, becoming more passionate about wine than any high-school student ought to be. By 1998, at twenty-two years old and fresh out of college, Gary was at the helm, rebranding the store from Shoppers Discount Liquors to Wine Library and launching a website to go along with it. At that time, winelibrary.com was one of the first e-commerce wine stores in the world. Through the site, along with grassroots marketing and a loyal local customer base, Vaynerchuk grew his family business from $3 million in annual revenue to $60 million over the next five years.

But that was just his first act.

In an interview, Vaynerchuk said, "On my thirtieth birthday, I was driving to New York from New Jersey, from the store. And I realized I was only 99 percent happy. That 1 percent made me change my entire life." It was time to pivot.

For his second act, Vaynerchuk set his sights on social media stardom. At the risk of spoiling the story, and in the words of the man himself, he *crushed it*. In 2006, he started Wine Library TV, one of the first video blogs, for which Gary filmed a thousand episodes over a five-year period. He parlayed his growing influence into TV appearances, media features, and eventually a book deal. He understood the potential of the internet and was elbows-deep from the outset, leveraging it to massive success.

Today, Vaynerchuk is known for his content around entrepreneurship and business. He's known for his books, his startlingly prescient insights, and his unwavering commitment to achieving his lifelong dream of buying the New York Jets. What he's not known for is wine. Despite wine-tasting videos being the foundation of his online brand beginning over fifteen years ago, these days, very few people think of wine when they think of Vaynerchuk, except as a footnote to his career. Therein lies the power of a well-executed pivot.

Vaynerchuk's personal history is both inspirational and aspirational, with all the trappings of a proper success story: it's got immigrant work ethic, entrepreneurial zeal, and a lackluster student rising to the top of his industry. Like with most such stories, if you look back at them, you might fool yourself into seeing a linear narrative, a straight line from past to present. But as any entrepreneur or Content Creator knows, success is never quite so straightforward. It has dips and curves, plateaus and pitfalls. And stories like Vaynerchuk's, which begin in one industry and lead somewhere entirely different, always include a series of pivots. Sometimes intentional, always impactful, and often incendiary, pivots are hinges in your story, shifting you from where you are to where you want to go.

RECOGNIZING STAGNATION

At the tail end of 2017, I found myself increasingly uninspired by the world of fitness—it no longer sparked my spirit or lit me up in the same way it once had. The whispers of longing for excitement and passion started off small and subtle; I could have almost missed them, but they steadily grew into an inescapable yell.

. . . *It's time for something else.*

Unfortunately, I felt totally stuck in not knowing what to do next. The common practice among fitness influencers at the time was to take one of a few paths: start a clothing line, found a supplement line, open a gym, or move onto higher-level fitness coaching. I didn't feel passionate about any of these. Doubt flooded my mind. *Will I have to make videos about my life forever? Maybe they're right; social media isn't a real job. What if I just stopped doing this altogether? But . . . I can't. I'm in too deep. My entire world would come crumbling down.*

One random Tuesday during a mindless Instagram scroll sesh, I came across a video of an interview with Lewis Howes—a business educator, entrepreneur, and podcaster. Howes casually mentioned a "mastermind for six- and seven-figure business owners to learn about business and help each other grow for an entire year together." I had absolutely *no clue* what that meant, but I felt drawn to it and applied immediately. Eagerly awaiting a response, I received a phone call the next day from Howes, who explained what the program entailed—including the price.

$30,000 for the year.

Wow. I'd never made an investment like that before.

Hell—just over a year prior, I was leaving Rhode Island as a new graduate working a waitressing job, unsure of what my future held. And now I was considering whether or not to drop $30k on a program I'd never heard of, run by a person I barely knew?

Yes. My answer was a resounding *yes.* I did have the resources available to pay, but more importantly, I knew it was the right decision to expand my horizons to figure out my next steps. The opening in-person event a few weeks later changed *everything* for me. I'd joined with the intention of finding ways to build or scale my fitness business and ideally reinvigorate my passion along the way. Instead, I realized the next phase of my career was to teach others. As I learned how to launch, market, and create my own offers, I saw the value in taking charge of my career as a true entrepreneur rather than relying on brand partnerships. Within a month, I knew that I wanted to help others create some of the freedom and opportunity I'd experienced.

For the first time in a long time, I could see the next steps in my future. This is where my *hard pivot* out of the fitness industry and into the business world would begin.

A year later, I sat across from Vaynerchuk in his Manhattan office, sharing the story of navigating my pivot—and detailing the resistance I'd been meeting along the way. Many people in my audience, along with many of my fellow Creators, viewed my shift into business coaching with judgmental eyes. Some felt I lacked qualifications and credibility; others simply didn't care for the new content I was creating or the new version of me who was creating it.

This is perfectly normal. I'll tell you, as Vaynerchuk and I discussed, it's nearly unavoidable.

As soon as you begin to pivot, you'll hear a lot of negative feedback from two different groups of people. The first group will be the people around you. There's definitely merit to the "crab-bucket theory," which is a mentality some people have if they don't want you to succeed, as it makes them feel poorly about their own place in life. But more commonly, many people in your inner circle who love you are typically protecting you from getting hurt or making a mistake, which can come across like they're not supportive of your dreams. This is true no matter who you are. When Vaynerchuk began Wine Library TV, he heard a lot of chatter from those in his camp. He was criticized for all the time he was spending on the project and subjected to some not-so-gentle ribbing, and he received quite a bit of "don't quit your day job" commentary.

The second group of people will be the crowd who will want you to stay in your box and will resent you for leaving that box. They'll come out with comments like "Stay in your lane" or "Get out of this space; you don't belong here." Both of these groups of people are usually projecting their own insecurities about their own life or struggles with change and growth onto you.

THE PIVOT

For Content Creators, the process of pivoting isn't just a simple process of creating different content. It may feel like an *identity crisis*. It's being watched, judged, criticized, and doubted while you leave behind an old version of yourself that other people—whom you may not even know—have come to follow, love, or rely upon. The repeated affirmation of your *social media persona* has probably been drilled into your community, no matter how big or small your audience size is. Everyone in your internet orbit has come to know you and your brand for what it's been up to that point. It's a clearly marked box, fixed and reliable. Your audience has willingly opted into *this* persona—and, as a result, may feel resistance to any shift away from that and toward another version. It's been said that a brand is a promise made over and over again; when a brand pivots, it can seem like that promise is being broken.

But every brand has at least one human behind it who has ever-evolving passions, interests, and parts of themselves they've yet to meet. As you live, you have new experiences, adventures, and ideas, all of which contribute to the ongoing evolution of your personality. In other words, you change, and you grow. That same box that you worked so hard to build can begin to feel like a prison. What seems solid and secure from the outside can feel stagnant and stifling on the inside. If you're a personal brand, you'll eventually find yourself contending with the pressure to stay in your lane and not change. Whether it's one of your clients advising you on which direction they think you should take your brand in or someone in your comments section saying you don't even deserve to have a following, prepare to meet varying levels of resistance, criticism, and pushback. If you've felt like you're merely acting out the persona you've created—almost as if you're faking it—in order to keep your audience satisfied and avoid rocking the boat, that's a clear indicator. It's time for the next stage on your journey: the *pivot.*

> Stepping into your pivot is a choice to leave the familiar behind and embark on a more uncertain road ahead—*and any further resistance to this process will only lead to more internal chaos.*

ACCEPTING YOUR PIVOT MEANS GRIEVING THE OLD YOU

For the first twelve months after deciding to pivot from fitness influencer to business coach, I attempted to maintain both brands and appease my audience. I was told to not give up on fitness because of what I'd built. It was seen as a wise business move to keep both, a solid backup option. Comments and messages poured in with feedback from audience members expressing their dislike and dissatisfaction with my choice. To this day, I still get asked if I'll ever make fitness videos again. I even started a new YouTube channel to separate my fitness content from my business content. I was living a double life.

I watched as my Instagram likes plummeted from a consistent twenty thousand or more per photo to under seven thousand almost overnight—which was a huge hit to my ego, reinforcing the self-doubt I already felt. At the time, I was the only person in my community of fitness influencers making this type of change, shining a bright light onto my every move. The judgment and criticism I received—not just from consumers but also from other fitness influencers—were unreal. *This must be like what celebrities feel when their breakups are all over the tabloids,* I thought. Everyone and their dog had an opinion about my life choices. I had a newfound respect for and understanding of the stresses and pressures of the ultra-famous.

Stepping into this "new me" felt like a baby deer trying to walk for the first time—awkwardly stumbling, easily startled, and not sure where to take my next step. I was trying to figure out who I was *and* convince everyone that I knew what I was doing. I couldn't let this fail, and I wanted the change to be worth it. I was determined to prove everyone wrong—including myself. This desire welcomed an intense drive to learn, a yearning to become the "expert" so I could move on from the awkwardness, not feel like an idiot, and build success as quickly as possible.

In hindsight, I can see that each of these experiences was a part of the grieving process that my audience and I had to go through. There was shock, denial, anger, bargaining, depression, detachment, and more in my story. It's far more common than you'd expect.

But as painful as it sounds, there was *magic* in the mess of it all. I learned to trust my own intuition regardless of the doubt and pressure that arises when other people have their own ideas of what they want me to do. I had to accept myself even more fully, even though it could've been easier to people-please and hide from what I *truly* wanted—and who I *truly* was. The next stage of my journey in the business world did more for me than I could have ever imagined, and it was *exactly* what I had to do.

Pivoting takes bravery, courage, and vulnerability. You're letting yourself be seen as the caterpillar before you transition into a butterfly. As a Content Creator, think about this as a *learning opportunity* to understand yourself on a deeper level. When you reinvent yourself, innovate on what you've built, and let go of the predictability of the past, you are in the process of meeting new parts of yourself.

WHY LOSING FOLLOWERS IS *AWESOME*

The thought of losing followers may set in motion a lot of fear for Content Creators—especially if you've been publicly vulnerable on your platform. It may be experienced as a highly personal attack on one's character, a threat to one's livelihood, or a rejection of you as a person. This may be exacerbated even further for those with PTSD, trauma, abandonment wounds, and rejection wounds. If you've ever felt emotionally distraught or dysregulated after losing followers, it doesn't mean you're vain or self-centered; it just means the loss of followers has likely triggered a deeper wound within you.

If you've experienced any kind of reaction that's creating a significant difficulty for you, please see a professional for support. Your mental health *is* important, the impact *is* real, and social media triggers *are* a very real and valid place where traumas can get reactivated. But if you've received the support you need or your activation is simply more uncomfortable than it is destabilizing, a simple shift in perspective can help you in seeing that losing followers is actually for your benefit.

Followers will come and go for reasons that have absolutely nothing to do with you. Living your life to its fullest, following your authentic desires, and being true to yourself will naturally attract people who are on a similar frequency and repel people who are on different frequencies. This is the same process of how we vibe and connect with friends in real life and how other people might be nice but not our flavor. The loss of followers simply means—for whatever reason—you and those followers are on different frequencies now and it's time for a change. It doesn't mean you won't be successful and attract new followers or that you've done anything wrong. It's just a change in frequencies.

> "I like getting unfollowed because my growth and expression of myself as a human means way more to me than 'preparing' content for you to like! I purposely follow people I disagree with because, to me, it's the greatest form of learning."
>
> SHAUN T, CELEBRITY TRAINER AT BEACHBODY, PODCASTER, AND ENTREPRENEUR

I don't necessarily believe that people leaving your orbit "makes room" for people who are a "yes" for you, but I do believe it helps you become more and more clear about who you are—which refines and enhances your magnetism over time.

followed

TYPES OF PIVOTS

Some pivots are massive, while others are small and subtle. All pivots will shift your brand into being more attractive to some and more repellent to others, and they ultimately provide you the opportunity for both audience refinement and audience expansion. The type of pivot you make will have its own type of trajectory. Below are the four different types of pivots you may find yourself making.

Expansion Pivot

The expansion pivot is a horizontal move where you maintain your current industry, expertise, and core brand message while adding more topics or formats to expand your breadth and reach. This is what you'd think of as a typical brand path in one core direction. Even the subtlest of shifts can have a major impact on the perception of your brand.

Any Content Creator who has had children and shared parts of that experience online knows what it feels like to have so much of their brand change as a result. Perhaps you've added videos like "Light seated yoga flow—third trimester" to your YouTube yoga brand. This may seem like a simple shift, but it attracts (and repels) an entirely different audience of people who can relate to the intersection between pregnancy, children, and yoga. Expansion pivots are incredible for creating a legacy: your audience follows your work for years, and you become deeply solidified in your niche as the go-to person for the topics you discuss, while still adding freshness to what you do by making small adjustments throughout the lifetime of your brand. If you've found a great formula and what you're doing is working—stick with it!

Here are some examples of expansion pivots:

- Adding the topic of menstrual cycles to your already thriving feminine-wellness brand

- Dating someone new and sharing aspects of your relationship within your brand
- Adding in physical products to your digital brand that your audience comes to know and love

Shift Pivot

In 2017, my content went from workout and nutrition videos to topics like growing your audience and onboarding new clients. This was a shift pivot, a horizontal move from one industry to another. This kind of pivot changed my whole brand: the topics I talked about, the products I sold, and the types of clients and audience members I was attracting. The shifts were foundational, which very much affected my engagement and audience satisfaction for at least a year. Thousands of audience members unfollowed me at rapid rates, but even now, new audience members continue to find my new page and follow me every single day. Along with that, original audience members who followed me for fitness but found my business content aligned with where they were headed have stuck with me through this.

This kind of pivot requires your audience to shift how they relate to you in their minds—and it may take a long time for that to happen. As much as your pivot is about you and your growth, the online business and branding world reminds us that executing on our pivot is also about taking our audiences along for that ride in a way that makes sense to them. How deeply entrenched your old brand is in the eyes, minds, and hearts of your audience will affect how quickly you can pivot into your new brand.

I personally found it fairly challenging to shift my YouTube brand when I went from fitness to business, to the point where I ended up just allowing my YouTube channel to fizzle out altogether. I found it was better to focus on Instagram, building a new email list and starting a podcast for my business content.

Here are some examples of shift pivots:

- Ending your work helping people with body transformation and starting to help people with emotional transformation
- Discussing sexuality for Christian couples on Instagram after you've spent years as a nurse
- Transforming your page from travel to family after becoming pregnant and wanting to settle down

Daniel Radcliffe—best known as the actor who played Harry Potter from ages eleven to twenty-two—is a great example of someone who's had a brand identity so deeply entrenched in the minds of his fans that it's been challenging for him to break out into non–Harry Potter acting roles. In the most recent Harry Potter twenty-year reunion special on HBO Max, Radcliffe even mentioned that he wasn't sure where Daniel began and Harry ended. Miley Cyrus (and many other Disney Channel child actors) pivoted from a wholesome TV character to a more rebellious and sexually liberated adult musician, exemplifying her own shift pivot.

Although they may take time and effort, shift pivots can work extremely well if you've already established a relationship with your audience where they like you for you—no matter what you do. Your true fans will stay to support and follow your journey, even though many others will fall off the "you" wagon. After you've gone through a shift pivot, you can consider expansion, escalation, or deepening pivots.

Escalation Pivot

With an escalation pivot, you maintain your current industry, expertise, and core brand essence while gaining more credibility, exposure, and PR for your brand through different mediums.

John Mulaney initially started his career as an assistant at Comedy Central in 2004, followed by a job in comedic writing at *Saturday Night Live* in 2008. Eventually, he escalated to having a very successful stand-up comedy career—most notably evidenced by his three stand-up specials: *Kid Gorgeous*,

New in Town, and *The Comeback Kid*. Throughout his career, Mulaney has stayed in the industry of comedy and has simply increased his credibility, exposure, and notoriety through different mediums. This is an example of an escalation pivot; you're essentially climbing the ladder in your industry, focusing on becoming either the biggest of experts, the most famous of entertainers, or the most popular of influencers. This requires commitment to mastery of one or two core skills in your craft, industry, or niche.

Here are some examples of escalation pivots:

- Starting a TikTok for your chiropractic brand and having a different part of your personality thrive in that format, growing your audience bigger than you ever have
- Writing a book as a YouTuber and having that book add tons of notoriety and authority to your already thriving and entertaining influencer brand
- Collaborating with other brands and partners to amplify visibility of your brand

Deepening Pivot

A deepening pivot is where you focus on squeezing the juice out of your current industry, expertise, and core brand message by solving more nuanced problems for your audience through more specificity. This style of pivot works best for those who want to become a specialist in their space. If you're an educator, this could look like gaining more certifications, doing more training, or studying more varied topics—making you highly credible and particularly useful to people who could benefit from your knowledge. If you're a cosplayer, this could look like dressing as niche characters with extremely detailed accessories and makeup. If you're in the beauty space, this could look like going to cosmetology school and subsequently working with people with a specific skin issue you specialize in helping to heal and creating content around that. In order to access the kind of information you have, people would have to dive into the depths of your area of expertise to obtain it. People will come to follow you for more specifics and specialties rather than *generalities* that hit the mainstream. Deepening pivots are great for you if you feel very strongly about your current niche and are drawn to helping your audience members with more nuanced situations that require an expanded skill set.

Here are some examples of deepening pivots:

- Reading more peer-reviewed research studies within the area of supporting postpartum depression
- Making extremely niche references about the cosplay community's antics
- Earning more certifications or degrees and sharing more detailed content in the area of physical therapy
- Becoming well studied in various wellness topics like biohacking, hormone balancing, Chinese medicine, energy work, Ayurveda, and more—allowing you to share very specific content

THE STAGES OF A PIVOT

Any type of pivot, no matter the size, will be a nonlinear, unpredictable process. Just like building a business, navigating a relationship, or embarking on a personal-development journey, we can only prepare ourselves so much for the inevitable trials and tribulations of what may happen. Every time I've pivoted, it's required a strong level of surrender and trust that I'm doing what's best for me—because the next chapter wasn't laid out perfectly for me. Surrender is being okay with sitting in the discomfort of the unknown and trusting that all will be okay even when it feels uncertain.

It will probably be hard, but *how* hard? You'll probably lose followers—but *how* will you feel about that when it happens? People will probably be upset—but *how* upset, and in what ways? You will probably succeed and feel better than ever—but *how* long will it take to see results?

The uncertainty is inescapable, but what can help ease some of your anxiety is knowing that there are many people out there *just* like you: feeling the same way, struggling with the same challenges. In my experience as both a coach who's helped hundreds of people make pivots and a Content Creator who has pivoted multiple times, there are patterns of cycles you'll be flowing in and out of during your journey to fully embodying the next stage of your brand identity. Let's look at those stages a little more closely!

Stage 1: Personal Transformation

Every pivot begins with a shift in your personal life: one that moves you, changes you, and creates a newfound sense of meaning that you cannot help but transfer over to your brand. I've seen countless Creators place that emergent, passionate, excited energy into their social media content, either intentionally or unintentionally. Maybe you moved to a new city, and you've found so much meaning in that new environment that you decided to make content about it. Perhaps you've endured a lot of challenges in relation to your health, so you found a passion in alternative modalities of healing—and sharing that *naturally* became a part of your brand. Or maybe you just knew you were ready to say more, so you decided to shift from posting photos only to making diverse content including graphics, carousels, articles, and longer-form content.

What you're going through in your personal life is likely to influence and shift your personal brand in the future, and in knowing that, here are two things to remember during this personal-life shift:

1. **Allow yourself to experience every aspect of this personal shift on your own terms.** You don't need to share any changes immediately—especially if it's vulnerable or tender or affects other people. This doesn't make you inauthentic or fake; it makes you someone who is processing the changes of your life! Give yourself plenty of offline space to allow this growth to happen. You may find

your future self thanking you for waiting until you fully processed your shift and felt like the new you had landed before making or sharing any big, life-changing decisions.

2. **It's entirely up to you to decide how much of this personal shift you want to explore integrating into your brand and content.** It could be that you keep a part of your life entirely to yourself—and the shift doesn't directly translate into how-to videos or a whole new brand. You are the sole steward of how you allow your life changes to affect your brand changes. Either way, the more you grow, the more your content will subtly shift, regardless of your active participation in making that happen.

Stage 2: Storytelling

> "Sometimes reality is too complex. Stories give it form."
>
> JEAN-LUC GODARD

As you are in the process of changing, growing, and shifting, stories are what will help walk your audience alongside you on your path. Put yourself in their shoes: they're making inferences and interpretations of who you are and what they can expect from you based on what you share. When you tell them a story—regardless of what format you choose to tell it in—they can actually contextualize all of the future changes to your content.

If you've gone through an epic spiritual awakening and immediately create an educational video about spiritual awakenings, it'll lack context, and your audience may feel confused or out of the loop. Telling the *story* of your spiritual awakening, however, will help them understand why you will create more spiritual content in the future. You'll find that when you tell stories, they act as bridges between worlds so that your audience can relate, build trust, and connect to you emotionally. They'll get to experience themselves through your story, vis-à-vis the threads of humanity you represent.

Share the stories of what's changed you—the inciting event, the resistance you felt, the trials and tribulations you went through, and the teachable moment for you. This way, you don't need to try to be an "authority" or "expert" to show up as a teacher. They'll learn through the story.

Stage 3: Mentorship or Formal Education

When I began sharing my workouts and meals on social media, I'd get messages every day with questions about how I was losing weight and changing my body. Luckily, I had an incredible fitness coach—William Grazione of The Educated Dieter—who became my fitness and nutrition mentor and was willing to help me answer the questions I was receiving from my growing audience of followers. I hadn't planned on becoming a personal trainer or nutrition coach, but I had to put that hat on when I gained hundreds of thousands of followers online.

This is where the internet can become tricky for Content Creators, and content consumers, too. There are millions of people out there creating content and doing their absolute best to answer questions people have, even though they're simply sharing their personal journeys and experiences. They never intended to become well-educated experts and may not be aware of the impact of what can happen when people take advice without personalized context.

Misinformation spreads, people take action without consulting their doctors or professionals, and uneducated Content Creators continue to be positioned as authority figures on the topics they talk about. Some people will actively position themselves as an authority (even if they aren't one). The engagement, notoriety, money, and success that come from claiming to be an authority would tempt many people. Social media has created a world where anyone can truly say anything, and people will believe them without much hesitation.

As mentioned in chapter nine, the Dunning–Kruger effect shows us that when we're learning about a new topic, we can feel a false sense of confidence in ourselves about how much we actually know. There's a moment of realization that soon afterward arrives once we discover we don't know shit. We begin to see how much there is to learn; we realize the importance of respecting the experts who came before us and the process of deeply integrating the information to minimize potential misinformation being spread and inadvertent harm being caused.

The best way to equip yourself when you're pivoting into a new space is to receive some kind of formal education, training, or mentorship on the topics you're going to talk about. It doesn't matter how big your following is—people *will* listen to you, and that's a big responsibility. It's all about the honor system on the internet—so as a Content Creator, adopt the values of integrity and personal responsibility. Keep learning. Know the impact of what you say *before* you speak. Consider different perspectives and possibilities before you share. Know the potential risks of what you share. Add disclaimers and trigger warnings to your content if there's a possibility that what you say will cause harm. Let yourself be a student, and tell your audience when you're still learning.

Stage 4: Repeat Stages 3 through 6 of the 9 Stages of Personal Branding

On a branding level, you'll need to retrain your audience to meet, know, and fully understand the "new" version of you. This may look like:

- Defining new words and language your audience may not understand yet or be familiar with to set the contextual landscape
- Introducing new concepts and information in simple, easy-to-understand ways
- Showing yourself living your new brand through embodying that version of you

It may feel like you're starting all over again, depending on the kind of pivot you're going through. Think of this as an opportunity to relearn yourself and your brand with new, fresh eyes. You may find yourself getting inspired by other people's content (Imitation Stage), slowly beginning to see the new "you" fit in (Awareness Stage), and testing and experimenting until you start gaining momentum (Confidently Crushing Stage). Eventually, you'll feel grounded and stable in your new brand (Full-Blown Branded Stage).

Stage 5: Developing New Skills

For so long, I felt scared to lead guided meditations with my clients—but knew I wanted to become skilled at leading them. I started off by writing meditations out word for word, slowly reading my words off the paper in front of me. Fast-forward to one year later: I found myself speaking on a stage in front of a 150-entrepreneur event, ready to lead a fifteen-minute meditation I had practiced and memorized. Unfortunately, my talk ran late, and I wasn't able to do the full meditation. The event host waved at me from the front row, with a hand-cutting-across-his-neck motion, signaling me to cut my talk short. I decided to cut the meditation down to five minutes and made up an entirely new meditation on the spot. No one had any idea, and many mentioned later that they enjoyed and loved that part of the talk the most!

A teacher becomes a *master* by hammering on their craft. In the book *Outliers*, Malcolm Gladwell writes that "ten thousand hours is the magic number of greatness." So write. Create. Record. Edit. Practice the new skills you're looking to embody both as a Content Creator and in your area of expertise. Let yourself experiment and practice.

> "In fact, researchers have settled on what they believe is the magic number for true expertise: ten thousand hours."
>
> MALCOLM GLADWELL, *OUTLIERS: THE STORY OF SUCCESS*

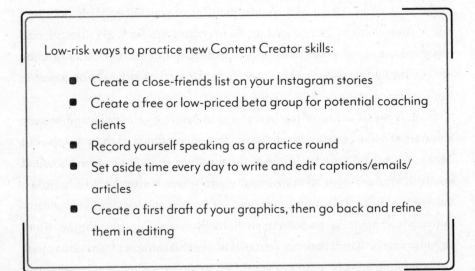

Low-risk ways to practice new Content Creator skills:

- Create a close-friends list on your Instagram stories
- Create a free or low-priced beta group for potential coaching clients
- Record yourself speaking as a practice round
- Set aside time every day to write and edit captions/emails/articles
- Create a first draft of your graphics, then go back and refine them in editing

Stage 6: Developing Mastery and Indoctrinating Your Audience

Want an insider's take on the experts you follow on social media?

Some of them showed up to social media with mastery of their craft. Some of them showed up as fully healed beings, ready to share the wisdom of their life. But *most* of them? They are sharing their content as an act of mastering their craft. Mastering their pain. Mastering their fears. It's a journey of learning *through* practice and experience.

If you've ever seen someone post a picture of themselves with their shirt off and thought, *Damn, they must feel perfectly confident in their body!* or seen someone post a piece of content about setting boundaries and reflected, *Wow, they must expertly set boundaries with ease in real life!*—you are mistaken. It's not to say that you're being duped by people who claim to be perfect; it's that we tend to believe that the people who share themselves publicly in a particular way have it *all* figured out. The truth is, *everyone* is in a constant state of figuring it out. Being able to post pictures of yourself publicly does represent a level of self-confidence but doesn't paint the *entire* picture. Sharing expert advice about boundaries does represent an intellectual understanding of boundaries but doesn't always speak to the level of *embodiment* a person has in their own life.

Social media is one of the best places to practice your skills and become a master of your craft *and* your story. The opportunity to show up to your "practice" every single day is one of the ways you can get your ten thousand hours. If you show up to your social media space with a level of humility, understanding of your limitations, and transparency with what you're learning versus what you've embodied, you'll likely be a net positive for the world, helping people. We all have unconscious biases and things to learn, so as much as it's important to be aware of spreading misinformation or how what you say may affect other people, it's almost impossible to be aware of *everything.*

Develop mastery offline, but also use your online presence to hammer down on your craft, your language, and your performance. Go record that meditation for your Instagram stories as a way to hold yourself accountable. Go record that podcast about your story as a way to practice the way you share and speak about it. Go teach that lesson to help your audience understand that topic, which will also help you understand them more and more each time you create.

- followed

Stage 7: Embodiment

All of the critical comments, stressful feedback, identity crises, self-doubt, imposter syndrome, and grief will be well worth it when, one day, you find that all of that seems to dissipate. When you find yourself confident in your ability to create engaging content, purposeful with your message, unbothered by judgmental comments, and reaching the audience members who your pivot has either impacted, helped, or entertained. When you barely have to try to succeed at this level because all of these skills are just . . . yours. *This is embodiment.* Your change is just who you are now. And the feeling you get when you've stayed on *your* path and cut out all the noise in your mind and from others who chose to have a negative opinion—it's priceless.

THE ONLY WAY OUT IS THROUGH

The challenges of being amidst a pivot include being seen during the vulnerable in-between space in front of your audience, losing some followers, feeling the need to explain yourself, and letting go of control of how you're perceived, but these are all opportunities to meet yourself more fully. There's also the chance to take *inspired action* and trust yourself more fully as the new version of you. Not everyone will understand you and your choices, and that may have you questioning whether all the effort of making the pivot is worth it.

Trust me—*it will be.*

There is no going back or "un-knowing" what the next step in your growth journey is. The sooner you stop fighting and make peace with it, the sooner you'll reap the benefits of who you get to become as a result of going through this process. The only way out is through all the judgment, questioning, and confusion, both from others and yourself. People will praise you, validate you, and share how your brand has impacted their lives. Others will vehemently reject the "new you." One will inflate your ego; one will deflate your ego. Don't forget that these opinions, comments, and judgments are just mirrors for you to accept and claim more of who you are—while simultaneously challenging those followers to take a deeper look at themselves (if they choose to do that!). Whether you choose not to have kids, want to get cosmetic surgery, or decide to change which style of eating you practice, who you hang out with, where you move, what relationships you start (or end), or which businesses you run—there will *always* be someone who will have a reaction and take it personally. Keep in mind that other people's opinions of you have nothing to do with you.

Your existence will be confronting no matter what you choose to do. To some people out there, your very presence might stir up emotion within them, saying much more about them than it does about you. So long as you're not harming anyone, let people say and think what they want. Allow your existence to shake up the status quo and incite change within others. And remember: how people perceive you isn't in your control.

twelve

Monetizing Your Social Media Presence

There is no shortage of books and courses intended to teach you how to make money online—but this is not one of them. As you've no doubt seen by now, *Followed* is not about the ins and outs of any aspect of living your life online, including the ways your presence on any platform can be monetized. It is about using your social media space to help you grow, actualize your potential, and, along the way, transmute that experience into all types of success—which can, of course, include reward. Before anything else, it's important to realize there are other types of currency than cash. The lessons you learn and the ways they help you grow as a person are rewards unto themselves, certainly, and influence is, in its own way, rewarding—even if you don't do anything with it directly. Knowing that people care about what you say and are somehow made better by hearing it is, for many of us, inherently and deeply fulfilling. But there are external rewards as well, and the more effectively you pursue the former, the more you're likely to receive the latter.

Gary Vaynerchuk wisely said: no matter what business you're in, we're all in the eyeballs business. With your platform and the exposure along with it come influence, impact, and, often, income. Even if you aren't being directly paid through sales, promotion, or other types of monetization, you can still receive all manner of incentive and rewards: discounts on products, free stays in hotels, free stuff showing up at your door, and access. Access is, perhaps, the biggest and most intangible type of reward. Getting people invested in your personal brand and growing that to whatever extent is a type of fame, and fame gives people access. Fame is a type of currency. It can be as simple as skipping a line and getting into the club, or it can mean being invited to parties and awards shows. All of these possibilities are beyond the scope of what I'm talking about here, but they do exist.

One of the best assets you can build for your long-term earning potential is a personal brand in which people are invested. Whether you're an entrepreneur creating content to market your business or a Creator getting paid by brands for user-generated content or doing multiple affiliate deals and sponsorships to generate revenue, getting paid to add value and be yourself is a dream you can make a reality. A brand that becomes memorable in the lives of your audience is one that has strong influence and staying power—even if you shift your industry, niche, or brand over time. It could be the way you do hair and help people experience beauty, the way you jump out of planes and help people feel inspired to live life to the fullest, or the movement you create by educating people on adult acne—when your brand impacts people, many of them will be followers for a very long time. The people who want more of what you have to offer will become customers, clients, or even simply a marker of your credibility, leaving you with the opportunity to earn more than you could ever imagine.

In 2013, twenty-year-old Florida native Bianca Taylor (@biancataylorm on Instagram) began sharing her experience of transitioning into veganism while on her fitness journey. Taylor documented how she trained and ate, and she shared her perspective on the importance of ending animal cruelty. Her passion provided a perfect window into personal experience, creating an opportunity for resonance and connection. Within six months, she'd attracted nearly five thousand followers to her account. Within a year, it was ten thousand. By 2019, Taylor's Instagram had grown to well over half a million followers, and she monetized in different ways—most notably by starting three companies: Bianca Taylor Fitness (fitness coaching for women, 2015), Vegan Fitness (fitness coaching with vegan nutrition, 2018), and Vedge Nutrition (sports supplements, 2018). But as her audience grew, so, too, did her interests. While Taylor has continued to create content about fitness and veganism through both her personal brand and her companies' additional social accounts, she has also shared sexier content online, including pole-dance videos and twerk tutorials. Her audience loved that content, and she absolutely loved creating it—which is when she decided to start an OnlyFans account, from which she'd go on to make over seven figures throughout her time as a paid Creator. Taylor's brand represents activism, body confidence, and sexual liberation. Although many of her fans who subscribed to her OnlyFans were men who paid for her "spicy" content, thousands of women consistently asked her things like "How did you become so confident? How can I build a brand like you and make money from my multiple different passions?" In 2020, Taylor birthed another company, The Embodied Babe, which helps women across the world find freedom in their lives and bodies through sexual empowerment, body confidence, and business coaching. Not only has Taylor started multiple successful six- and seven-figure companies and revenue streams, but she's also been a paid speaker for events across the world, a host for various in-person luxury retreats, and a paid influencer by many brands to promote their products. Taylor is the epitome of a multi-passionate Creator finding a place for all her passions by monetizing in multiple ways.

"When you're a content creator, you are an entrepreneur in the sense that you work for yourself, and create something out of nothing. There are also now many entrepreneurs who are content creators as well. These two professions go great together, as one feeds the other. If you have an engaged audience, you can transform some of that into customers, and vice versa.

But content creators are first and foremost, *communicators*. Their job is to create content for a living. And just as there are different entrepreneurs, working in different industries—there are different content creators, working in different mediums (video, text, audio, visual)."

SERGEY FALDIN

Each Creator has to find their own balance of what monetization styles allow them to create in a way that feels right to them. For some, that looks like creating art (e.g., paintings, products, books, NFTs, photos) and selling it directly to their audience. For others, it looks like working directly with brands and getting paid for creative skills and services—like those who are copywriters, videographers, influencers, and speakers. And, of course, for many, content creation has become a jumping-off point to starting your own business. Let's dive into the different ways you can generate income as a social media Content Creator.

MONETIZE DIRECTLY THROUGH THE PLATFORMS ON WHICH YOU CREATE

Some social media platforms—most notably, YouTube's AdSense program—pay their Creators directly through the platform by monetizing content with advertisements. By offering Creators the option to click "Monetize," Creators earn money based on an algorithmic breakdown of the number of views, total watch time, overall reach, and other supporting metrics of success that benefit the Creator, platform, and advertisers.

On the YouTube Creators channel, one of its monetization strategists, Stefan, says, "Before you can earn money on your channel, you need an audience. Now, to build an audience, you need to make consistent videos that viewers *really* like watching. And, like anything on YouTube, it's important that your videos follow YouTube's Community Guidelines. After that's all working for you, you can apply to join the YouTube Partner Program."[13] Each platform will have its own requirements to qualify for monetization, but it's well worth the extra effort if you're consistently creating content people enjoy watching anyway. Your creativity drives traffic and attention to their platform, and you should get paid for the skills you've cultivated and the time you've put in. Creating engaging content that viewers come back to consistently consume is a skill that can be honed and refined over time—if you have the will to work on it. As time goes on and social media platforms continue to compete for the attention of their users, more opportunities for direct monetization will likely pop up to incentivize Creators. To start, check out the Creator policies on YouTube, TikTok, Snapchat, Instagram, and

Twitch. This is a growing industry, and platforms will continue to find new ways to incentivize creators that will evolve with time.

If you have a smaller platform, post less consistently, or don't see yourself being a Creator that focuses on views and audience size as much, you'll be limited in how much you can make from the platforms' monetizing structures alone. There's definitely money to be made through direct monetization, but the bigger ocean of potential revenue streams comes from the other business avenues you can choose to pursue with your personal platform. We'll look at what all those potential revenue streams are in the next section.

Put Exclusive Content Behind a Paywall

If you're a Creator looking to be paid for your work and efforts, consider creating a membership platform space that allows you to create premium content behind a paywall. Some platforms lend themselves to sharing written and visual content, like Patreon, OnlyFans, Substack, and Medium. Others are fantastic for online courses and packaged information, like Kajabi, Teachable, and Thinkific. Others are amazing for music and podcasts, like Spotify and Anchor. Each platform has its own benefits and features that suit different styles of content, but what they all have in common is the ability to charge a subscription fee and upload the content within the membership area. In return for this subscription fee, subscribers will get exclusive access to specifically curated content not shared anywhere else. You can even create multiple tiers, offering varying levels of value and access for different rates. This kind of format allows you to pour your creativity into a space where people can enjoy it whenever you want to create. Within those spaces, you can create digital courses and premium video and photo content, communicate directly with members, schedule events and live streams, and create a community. Not only that, but Creators often experience an increased sense of comfort and freedom to share exactly what they want when members are choosing to be there and financially investing, including (but not limited to) personal life details and taboo or controversial topics. Think of this like your innermost circle!

Using a paywall style of monetization is great for you if you want to create exclusive content people typically want to pay for, especially on a frequent and regular basis. Think personal poetry, long-form articles with intensive research, spicy videos, live events and Q&As, educational topics, niche conversations, book clubs, art, and podcasts. If content creation itself is your jam, and you want to get paid for your creative efforts outside of free social media spaces, this is an awesome opportunity for you. Selling exclusive content allows you to stand on your own as an independent Creator and put your focus on creating the exact kind of content you want, knowing that others are willing to pay for it.

When starting one of these communities or spaces, make sure you clarify exactly what members can expect from you, whether it's weekly videos, poetry, musings, or premium articles. Think about what *you* want to create and position the platform around the value of *that.* If you aren't clear on your vision just yet, start off with a simple space that has one really clear purpose—like offering advice on how to become a better copywriter or exchanging tips for improving your sex life in your marriage. Once you feel more confident and gain some momentum, you can always add new tiers or expand the context of your community space.

Partner with Brands and Companies to Create Content for Their Products

If you enjoy being a Content Creator whose audience can follow you for free, getting paid by brands is a fully accessible opportunity you might like to explore. Whether it's becoming an affiliate and making a commission on products you sell, getting paid per post, or getting hired by a company to create content for their brand, this is a fantastic option for so many Creators.

Types of Creators include

followed

- **Influencers:** The "traditional" influencer will have a range of paid posts, partnerships, brand deals, and affiliate deals. It's all about creating content on their personal page that promotes brands to their audience. It gets eyeballs on the company's product or service using that person's audience. This is great for those who already have an audience or niche that already looks like a particular company's ideal customer, as it will allow for a seamless fit. This works well for you if you love making content and want to help businesses or business owners with their content creation. You might not want to build your own business, but this way, you'll still have the freedom of an entrepreneur. You can get paid by a company but have flexibility in hours and location. For many, it's a dream opportunity to score—but for longevity's sake, it's best to align with brands that match your value, skills, and personal lifestyle. This can be anything from a one-time deal to a full-time, salaried position. Companies need to create content in the modern day, and Creators are becoming increasingly valuable.
- **Paid Creative:** This is where you can work for a brand and make content for it. This usually looks like creating written content such as articles, blogs, or other social media posts, or perhaps a video or other visual content such as TikToks, Reels, or infographics. This is a great fit for those who want to use their skills to help a business or brand but aren't interested in being the front or face of the brand. This category also includes paid videographers, photographers, writers, and graphic designers.
- **Content Creator:** In this type of role, you are the face of a company or brand and help create content that supports that particular brand or business. It could look like creating fitness videos and demonstrating exercises for a company's training program, or perhaps other educational or informational content. This type of role is great if you want a stable environment to develop your expertise and skills but

want to gain experience or exposure under the guidance of a larger company. It might not be such a great fit if you are wanting to develop your own personal brand with your own values and unique niche.

Create Your Own Products and/or Business

Imagine visiting a new city where one of your friends lives. On a scale of 1 to 10, how seriously would you take their recommendations on where to eat or explore? Even if this friend didn't have the same taste in food as you, you'd still value their recommendation more than that of Yelp, OpenTable, or a random online article.

This is the same power of influence and possibility you hold as a Content Creator and the *exact* asset you can leverage that millions of companies recognize as a valuable marketing tool. As a Creator who started as an influencer for other companies and then began building companies of my own, I can say this: *having your own products, services, platforms, and spaces is the ultimate form of freedom.*

To have a *monetizable* and *memorable* brand, you need to:

- Create content that's highly valuable to others
- Become a consistent, reliable resource in the lives of your followers
- Develop authority and credibility in your space
- Provide offerings people desire that solve a problem or add value

To create your own products and/or business, a *monetizable brand* is one of the many components needed. A built-in audience who is ready to buy can make revenue generation and customer acquisition easier, but as anyone who has endeavored into entrepreneurship knows: it's only one piece of the puzzle in the game of business.

Content Creators, if you're not building a business of your own, you can learn from this section by recognizing the power of strategy and structure. For a business to succeed, the company needs to determine:

followed

- Who its target customer is
- How its product serves a specific need in the market
- How to make its product stand out
- What the essence of its brand is
- Which channels it wants to build audiences on
- The key partners and team members required to keep it running
- What its operations are
- The infrastructure of how each department works together
- Other elements like finances, customer success, and company culture

The main difference between monetizing in other ways as a Content Creator and running a business is that content creation is typically a means to an end to market the business, not the main priority or focus. But regardless of what kind of entrepreneurial spirit you have, remember: figuring out how you're going to make money through the vehicle of these platforms is *up to you*. You can create physical products, educational products, services, coaching, a creative agency, media, or anything else that allows you to thrive as a creative entrepreneur! Maybe you have an Etsy shop, or have a hair salon, or do energy healings. The most important thing to remember about being a business owner is that the way you use social media gets to be guided by the needs of your business. There isn't any one "right" way to do it, and you can determine social media strategies that make sense for the kind of business you run.

The pursuit of making money online is your right. Get *after* it. Along that journey, you'll run into different bumps along the way—and while it's true that you can monetize just about anything, it's also true that you can keep some passions or interests as purely fun, free from the creative restrictions of monetization. For a brief moment in my journey, I felt overwhelmed with all the money I was "leaving on the table." The companies that were willing to pay me for posts, the people who were willing to affiliate my products, and the ideas I had for business ventures were endless. In fact, one of the main struggles I faced was letting go of my monthly salary from PEScience (a supplement company I worked with for years as a fitness influencer) when I pivoted away from fitness. But as I peeled back the layers of what money, content creation, social media, and growth all mean to me, I realized this:

> No amount of money is worth losing myself over—and I can create money in ways that support my soul and honor my values.

In your own pursuits of making money online: do your thing, figure it out, work to "make it"—whatever that means to you. Do what *you* have to do for yourself. And just remember to keep checking in on your creativity, playfulness, fulfillment, and soul.

conclusion

Let Your Journey Unfold

> "Maybe the journey isn't so much about becoming anything. Maybe it's about unbecoming everything that isn't you, so you can be who you were meant to be in the first place."
>
> —Paulo Coelho

Someone interviewing me for a podcast once asked: "If you'd never started a YouTube channel, what do you think you would be doing now?"

I took a very long pause, really thinking about what the answer could be when I realized—I didn't have one. Truthfully, I don't know where life would've taken me had I not stumbled upon social media and started creating content because my journey as a Creator has been where I've figured out who I am and what my greatest gifts are. I've had the opportunity to do so many things: film daily vlogs about my life, coach people across the world, and write about my experiences in fitness, business, relationships, sexuality, and more. I've found my best friends, traveled around the world, been paid by brands, joined incredible podcasts, and met so many other entrepreneurs and Creators who are also making a mark on the world through their authenticity. I got to build a business, make millions, meet my husband, and write a book!

Social media was and continues to be a portal for me. A portal to seeing myself, experiencing myself, and connecting with people who resonate with my content. Which begs the question: What versions of you are waiting to be met through your journey of being a Content Creator? Maybe a professionally produced podcast isn't in the cards for you, or perhaps you're not a viral dancing sensation. But . . . maybe you *are*. How can you be so sure without genuinely trying? How will you know if you never take the steps to allow for your true essence to reveal itself over time with each and every piece of content you post?

That's the *power* of social media.

No one knows exactly who they are when they start. We've all got our insecurities—the parts of ourselves we hide, don't want people to see, or feel embarrassed about. We've all got our strengths, too—the gifts, qualities, and skills we like to share, want to be seen for, and offer to the world. We won't always be everyone's cup of tea. If this book teaches you anything, let it be that being yourself is truly the only option. Finding the courage to share yourself vulnerably will only lead to becoming more unapologetic. The longer you're online, the more you can view social media as a vehicle to access more of your essence, and the more you can pay attention to the learning opportunities right in your face. Oh, shit. This is *it*. You've just found one of the most expansive playgrounds for growth ever designed.

Your exact background, experiences, skills, and interests are *exactly* what this world needs. So are your quirks, fears, and bits of humanity that feel messy. We're all incredibly hungry for authenticity—and you living your life out loud online is *exactly* the medicine you get to offer. If you have the courage to be your most embodied self, the world will bring you all the aligned people, places, and opportunities you could ever dream of. I've seen it with every client I've ever coached, and I *know* this can be your reality, too.

Remember:

Your most authentic self is unique and a gift to the world.

You have infinite potential awaiting, ready to be expressed.

Learn to trust your intuition—your inner guidance—even if it doesn't make logical sense.

Your inner-guidance system will take you along many different pathways as a Content Creator. You'll find yourself in situations that'll make you feel powerful—like having many people come to one of your live streams or when someone sends you a message saying how you changed their life. You'll also find yourself in situations you'll loathe entirely—like dealing with people projecting their insecurities onto you or having someone steal your original content. You'll find community, and you'll lose other friendships. You'll make money, and you'll leave money on the table. You might experience something traumatic, and you will probably experience things that are very healing. The magic is found through your inspired action and trust in the process. But you won't be done with your work there. You may experience increased pressure, a sense of responsibility, fear of failure, fear of success, a need to pivot, or even more imposter syndrome coming up. And yet again, you'll find yourself with the opportunity to meet more of yourself by learning to reaccess your center, your peace, your intuition, and your inner knowing to meet a new level of success.

At many points in your journey, you'll feel *over it all* and will desperately need a social media scrub and tech detox to clear out the noise. Sometimes, you'll feel bored, annoyed, and frustrated. Other times, you'll feel energized, curious, and creative. You'll find yourself in synchronicity and alignment with your audience. At various points, you may feel stuck or stagnant, wondering if social media is even for you anymore. None of these feelings are wrong. Your inner world is full of information, and it takes time to cultivate awareness of all that's happening in there and how to interpret it. Maybe you'll soon be ready to talk about your love of astrology or gardening or finally try out the latest social media platform that's new but piques your interest. Go for it all. Allow it to lead you into accessing new parts of yourself.

Remember—you can acknowledge your negative thoughts, investigate your wild desires, validate your own feelings, and interpret your next steps as best you can at *any* point in time. You won't always know the answer, and that's okay, too. For every shadow, there's an abandoned part of yourself waiting to be owned. Where there is creative resistance, there's a part of you yearning for more space, freedom, and flow. If you are feeling stuck in a plateau and angry at the latest algorithmic change . . . your next level of evolution is waiting for you. You're going to grow, change, shift, and evolve. It's not that parts of you will die or that you'll change in a negative way. It's more that you'll let go of what you never were in the first place and embody more of who you *truly* are.

The process of truly knowing yourself through social media won't always be immediate or linear. You get to grow at your own pace, and each new, scary experience allows for the next level of growth to occur. For me, starting to write content led me to find my voice and eventually write my first book. Building a business and coaching others showed me how to monetize my skills and become a leader to others. Getting publicly called out taught me how to strengthen my sense of self-worth, examine and educate myself on my own privileges, and ground myself in the face of judgment and projection. Pivoting from fitness to business allowed me to trust myself, my voice, and my path wholeheartedly. Every single season, experience, and lesson led to the creation of this book.

Followed may sit on the shelf for a while after your first read, and I love that for you. It'll be here for you whenever you hit a new wall and feel stuck. This isn't the kind of book you read once and forget about. It's there for your *entire* journey as a Content Creator. You can read any chapter you feel called to or pick it up when a new challenge arises. Think of this book like the secret weapon in your pocket, a loving and supportive guide from someone who's lived the experiences and learned the lessons so you get to experience the journey with eyes wide open, be bold and adventurous, and take many creative risks!

I'm so excited for the direction your life will take as you integrate each lesson for yourself (and there will be so many lessons!). Developing yourself through social media has the power to *completely transform* your life. I look at all the best things that came into my life as a result of putting myself out there—the people, the opportunities, the growth—and it's clear the risk was completely worth the reward. I know it'll be worth it for you, too.

This just leaves one question: What else will you learn from being followed?

resources

PART I: THE FOUNDATIONS OF BECOMING AN AUTHENTIC CONTENT CREATOR

Chapter 2–Embodying Your Inner Creator

- Julia Cameron, *The Artist's Way*
- Elizabeth Gilbert, *Big Magic*

Chapter 3–Are You Who They Think You Are?

- Tucker Max, *The Scribe Method*
- Huberman Labs Podcast
- Susan Cain, *Quiet: The Power of Introverts in a World That Can't Stop Talking*

Chapter 4–Keeping Up with the Influencers

- Dr. Robert Kegan's (former Harvard psychologist) *Theory of Adult Development*

- Philosophies:
    - Buddhism
    - Stoicism
- Mark Manson, *The Subtle Art of Not Giving a Fuck*

PART II: PROTECTING YOURSELF FROM THE DARK SIDE OF SOCIAL MEDIA

Chapter 5–Rewrite Your Social Media Narrative

- Marie Kondo, *The Life-Changing Magic of Tidying Up*

Chapter 6–The Link Between Trauma and Social Media

- Peter Levine, PhD, founder of *Somatic Experiencing*
- Mastin Kipp, *Claim Your Power*
- Bessel Van Derk Kolk, *The Body Keeps the Score*
- Helpful therapeutic modalities:
    - Somatic Therapy
    - EMDR
    - Internal Family Systems
    - Breathwork

Chapter 7–Embracing Your Social Media Shadow

- Jungian psychology
- Debbie Ford, *The Dark Side of the Light Chasers*

Chapter 8–Trolls, Haters, and Critics–*Oh My*!

- National Suicide Hotline: 1-800-273-8255
- Fucking Cancelled Podcast

PART III: BUILDING AN AUTHENTIC ONLINE BRAND

Chapter 9–The 9 Stages of Personal Branding

- Psychological Models of Development
  - Maslow's *Hierarchy of Needs*
  - Erik Erickson's *Stages of Psychosocial Development*
  - *Grave's Model/Spiral Dynamics*

Chapter 11–Niching Down into Yourself

- Netflix Documentary, *The Social Dilemma*

Chapter 10–Pivoting Powerfully

- Elizabeth Kubler-Ross, *On Death and Dying*

acknowledgments

To my mom, Linda, my dad, Tom, and my sister, Lindsey—thank you so much for always trusting me to choose what was best for me, even if it didn't make logical sense. The kind of encouragement, love, and acceptance you provided as I was growing up and figuring myself out made it that much easier to take risks and become the person I am today.

To my husband and life partner, John—you've been my number-one greatest cheerleader, support system, and teacher throughout this process. I appreciate all the support you've provided in making this book sing with beautiful sentences. Our shared love of finding the exact right words to describe the human experience is one of the great joys of my life, and your support does not go unappreciated. More importantly, you've sat with me during every difficult moment of vulnerability, through the gentle unraveling, and throughout my journey in becoming the woman I am today. You've helped create space for my depths so I can rise and become the leader I need to be in the world. John Romaniello, you are my best friend. I wouldn't want to do life with anyone else.

To my incredible research and writing assistant for this book, Karishma—I could not have done this without you. If I were to go back and dream up the perfect teammate for this project, I wouldn't even come close to describing you and the magic that is our relationship. From always being on the same workflow cycles all the way across the world, to having complementary human-design charts, to enjoying the beauty of being co-Creators and relishing the magic that has been creating this book—you're everything. Thank you for your depth of support in managing the book project, always knowing what's "wrong" with a section, having the best ideas, and being deeply devoted to the quality of your own writing and editing work.

To every single one of my friends in my community and chosen family—thank you for your deep support, love, *hype*, and validation during the long writing process. Seeing you get as excited about this book as I am (if not more) helped me keep writing, even when it was difficult. Your friendship, playfulness, depth, and joy has made my life so deeply fulfilling, giving me the energy I've needed to complete this project. Your love, loyalty, and energy are completely unmatched. Thank you.

To my agent, Wendy, and the incredible publishing team at BenBella—thank you for "getting it" and believing in this book from the get-go when many others didn't. It's been an absolute pleasure to work together to bring this book to life.

To Richelle Fredson, who supported me in forming the proposal for this book—Richelle, you also "got it" so quickly and did the up-front work to help me solidify my ideas into a beautifully formed structure. That process was so incredibly supportive in unscrambling my creative mind and putting these topics into the language they deserve.

To all my clients whom I've worked with over the years—thank you for allowing me to be your guide through the vulnerable experience of being an online Content Creator and entrepreneur. Thank you for trusting me to be a small part of your journey.

To my haters—thank you for helping me understand what it's like to be a Content Creator in the modern world and teaching me that it's okay to let people misunderstand you. Unsarcastically, I appreciate your pushback.

And finally, to anyone else who has followed me over the years—thank you for being in my digital orbit, staying connected to me, and allowing me to be a part of your life. We don't always have a direct relationship, but ours is special—because if you follow me, I know at least something about you. I know you're devoted to seeing and understanding who you truly are, and I respect and admire that. Let's all keep going.

notes

1. Julia Thomas, "What Is Ego Psychology?", BetterHelp, updated October 4, 2022, https://www.betterhelp.com/advice/psychologists/what-is-ego-psychology/.
2. Huberman Labs Podcast Episode 53: "The Science of Making and Breaking Habits."
3. Emily Stewart, "Why do we buy what we buy?", *Vox*, July 7, 2021, https://www.vox.com/the-goods/22547185/consumerism-competition-history-interview.
4. Natali Morad, "Part 1: How to Be an Adult—Kegan's Theory of Adult Development," Medium, September 28, 2017, https://medium.com/@NataliMorad/how-to-be-an-adult-kegans-theory-of-adult-development-d63f4311b553.
5. Somatic Experiencing About Page, Ergos Institute of Somatic Education, accessed November 3, 2022, https://www.somaticexperiencing.com/somatic-experiencing.
6. As Creators, it's incumbent upon us to both realize how our content has the potential to re-trigger those consuming it and protect them by offering a content warning (CW) or trigger warning (TW) to acknowledge the potentially sensitive content.
7. Research Overview Page, EMDR Institute, Inc., accessed November 3, 2022, https://www.emdr.com/research-overview/.
8. Camille Rainville, "Be A Lady They Said," Writings of a Furious Woman (blog), December 9, 2017, https://writingsofafuriouswoman.wordpress.com/2017/12/09/be-a-lady-they-said/.

9. "Compartmentalization," *Psychology Today*, accessed November 3, 2022, https://www.psychologytoday.com/us/basics/compartmentalization.
10. Amy Morin, "This Is How Your Thoughts Become Your Reality," *Forbes*, June 15, 2016, https://www.forbes.com/sites/amymorin/2016/06/15/this-is-how-your-thoughts-become-your-reality/#36e32c9b528a.
11. "Parasocial Relationships: The Nature of Celebrity Fascinations," www.findapsychologist.org, National Register of Health Service Psychologists, accessed November 3, 2022, https://www.findapsychologist.org/parasocial-relationships-the-nature-of-celebrity-fascinations/.
12. NVC Consulting, "What Is Spiral Dynamics®?", Spiral Dynamics, accessed November 28, 2022, https://spiraldynamics.org/about/what/.
13. "Intro to Making Money on YouTube," YouTube Creators, January 22, 2019, YouTube video, 3:22, https://youtu.be/bIngfKyJyUw.

index

S

about the author

Amanda Bucci is an entrepreneur, speaker, and Content Creator who helps people figure out what it means to be authentic. Since 2014, she's created hundreds of hours of video content to educate and entertain, published hundreds of thousands of words across her social media channels, and worked with clients ranging from first-year business owners to some of the most popular podcasters in the world. Amanda specializes in helping people through the emotional work and practical steps to living authentically in their businesses, lives, and relationships. She lives in Austin, Texas, with her husband, John, and their dog, Cooper. *Followed* is her first book.

Want to stay updated with Amanda's latest?
Follow her at www.amandabucci.com
@amandabucci